ITALIAN LITERATURE

COMPARATIVE LITERATURE series

English Literature: Defoe to the Victorians

In preparation

English Literature: The Twentieth Century
American Literature: The Nineteenth and Early Twentieth
Centuries
American Literature: The Twentieth Century
French Literature: The Nineteenth Century

Comparative Literature

ITALIAN LITERATURE
THE DOMINANT THEMES

Christopher Cairns

DAVID & CHARLES
Newton Abbot London Vancouver

BARNES & NOBLE
(a division of Harper & Row Publishers Inc)

for Alexander Dominick

ISBN 0 7153 7391 9 (Great Britain)
ISBN 0-06-490921-2 (United States)
Library of Congress Catalog Card Number: 76-24070

This edition first published in 1977
in Great Britain by
David & Charles (Publishers) Limited
Brunel House   Newton Abbot   Devon

First published in the USA by
Harper & Row Publishers Inc
Barnes & Noble Import Division

Published in Canada by
Douglas David & Charles Limited
1875 Welch Street   North Vancouver   BC

Set in 11 on 13pt Garamond
and printed in Great Britain
by Latimer Trend & Company Ltd Plymouth

Contents

Acknowledgements

I owe a debt of gratitude to several people in the preparation of this work, from the early discussions about whether a 'theme' can really be used as a categorisation, or way of sub-dividing literature, to valuable criticisms of individual sections by my colleagues and the tolerance of one generation of first-year students, ruthlessly exploited as guinea-pigs to assess the impact of one chapter on its prospective audience. Those colleagues will not perhaps always concur with my choice of themes and content-patterns as a way of looking at literature, but I have benefited greatly from discussions of my 'heresies' with them. I should like to thank the publishers for, above all, their patience, and active encouragement at all stages in the preparation of the work. And, of course, my wife. There is much about the Italians, implicit and explicit, in this book. She has defended her Italian compatriots through thick and thin against the assaults of Anglo-Saxon generalisations. Should they remain unrecognisable, it is my fault, not hers.

C.S.C.
Aberystwyth, January 1977

Preface

In proposing a survey of the main themes of Italian literature in modern times this book does not aspire to be a history of Italian literature. On the contrary, the narrowly chronological approach, with its apparatus of influences and debts to previous writers, has been specifically avoided. Nor does it propose to include every work of literature in an exhaustive encyclopedia of names and titles. Rather it attempts to describe the literature of the Italians under thematic headings.

The division into thematic chapters will produce some strange partners, entail some curious omissions and may admit the odd anachronism. But, these factors apart, the aim has been to collect into convenient divisions the significant literature of modern Italy that has mirrored the main themes of Italian civilisation, and to present that literature not in the context solely of a series of aesthetic currents but as the writing of the Italians, springing from the historical and geographical circumstances of the country. Necessarily, then, there will be as much of the Italians and their civilisations as there will be of books. Even if there are disappointments for the specialist and literary historian, it is hoped that the formula of literature in history, and the arrangement of literature by theme—the former an approach and the latter a series of pigeon-holes for convenience—will provide some new insights, a kind of historical coherence and a focus of interest for the reader whose attention may well have been drawn to the themes themselves in his reading of other literatures.

So the reader who is seeking a sophisticated philosophical analysis of Petrarch's *Africa* will not find it here. For posterity considers it a work of lesser importance than the *Canzoniere*. Rather he will find the figure of the poet as author of truly great love poems, and as thinker, writer and politician in fourteenth-century Italy. He will find perhaps a surprising modernity, a continuity and a link with the past in present-day attitudes. Every age has its philosophy and its civic values. Every age finds these values reflected as themes or content-patterns in its literature. Without wanting for a moment to impose the values of today on the literature of the past, it remains true that some of the enduring preoccupations of present-day Italians—politics, the Church and the state, economic and social change—have found their place in literature in the recent and distant past, and, as themes, have contributed to significant works in different ages and generations of writers. Consequently the criteria of choice and omission have been three: what sections of Italian literature define it as something particularly Italian in the values, ancient and modern, of Italian society? What Italian literature of the past has some demonstrable relationship with the Italians in their present? And what Italian literature is likely to reach the reader beginning the exploration of the subject in a reasonably accessible text?

There is one sense in which Italy stands apart from the mainstream of European literature. For even the phrase 'Italian literature' invites debate. Since unification under one flag in the nineteenth century, critics have often been tempted to impose a 'nationalism' on ages when the word means nothing, to use a chance mention of the word 'Italian' as an indication of deep stirrings of an Italian national conscience. It is hoped that this book will not betray Italian history for the convenience of thematic categories. By 'Italian literature' we mean literature in Italian, often, though not always, in that form of Tuscan which has become standard; but in this lies one of the most fertile fields for debate for Italians—the *Questione della lingua*. The consideration of medium for expression is part and parcel of literary 'motivation', of course, but in its concentration on themes or content-patterns this work does not deal in detail with the evolution of the Italian language.

In a sense, the best introduction to literature is a series of titles spoken with enthusiasm—in a word, an exhortation to read. 'Introductions' are no substitute for the works themselves. It is hoped, however, that the reader beginning the exploration of Italian literature will find a helpful orientation in the pages which follow and perhaps some points of comparison. Themes have something to say about the context of the works, their background and relationship with things outside writing, and about ways in which they are particularly *Italian*.

Finally, this book is concerned with the values of Italians today and their roots in the relatively recent past. This is not to deny the fundamental importance of medieval and Renaissance literature in Italy, but detailed consideration of these falls outside the scope of the present series. Accordingly, the great medieval Italian classics will find their place as part of 'The Italian Heritage' in the introductory chapter.

CHAPTER 1

The Italian Heritage

Any attempt to define in a general way the spirit of Italian literature in modern times cannot avoid two historical and geographical considerations of supreme importance: Italy was the home of classical Rome and remains to this day the centre of the Roman Catholic Church. It is almost impossible even today to participate in a discussion of Italian society and culture without touching on these central realities. In art, republican government and law, secular Rome stands at a crossroads in the history of the peninsula, just as Christian Rome occupies a commanding position in any consideration of theology, ethics and philosophy. And even this is far too simple. There is hardly any literary production of significance in Italy from the year 1300 to the present day in which the age-old dualism of papacy and empire—or its modern equivalent, Church and state—is not present.

The very geographical position of the peninsula gives hints of the dramas of Italian history and literature. Jutting out into the Mediterranean from the main land mass of Europe, the long boot of Italy faces North Africa and the Near East, bounded, as it were, by Spain and the Dalmatian coast. Looking to the west, the Italian finds the rival Latin cultures of France and Spain. In the east Italy borders on Yugoslavia with Albania farther south. For long the area to the east—the home of the Turkish empire at Constantinople—presented a threat to Christendom, while at the east-west hinge Venice had been the great maritime and commercial republic down to the end of the eighteenth century. Bound in the north by that great natural frontier, the Alps, Italy has always been cut off, in a sense, from the currents of central and western Europe. So the position of the peninsula is symbolic of the central realities of Italian history. Thrust perilously out into the Mediterranean Sea, Italy was to enjoy the riches of a trade link between east and west and suffer the disadvantages of holding the balance between Christianity and Islam.

The attractions of the land were one of the reasons why Italy remained divided for much of the period of her history under discussion. Her sunny slopes and fertile valleys were constantly the prize for the invader from the north; even the papal state, in its moments of political crisis, thrived on the disunity of the Italian states aided by the variable Catholic consciences of the French and the Germans. Unity under one flag came only in the nineteenth century, although in cultural terms linguistic affinities had been present since the Roman Empire.

But if we want to understand one of the great literatures of Europe, we must narrow our focus a little and look more closely at the Italy of modern times. The country emerges as a land of sharp contrasts. For it was not aspirations to unity, but the *separateness* of the Italians that was to aid in the formation of Dante and Petrarch; it was the world of patronage in *courts*, not republics, that was to throw up Ariosto in Ferrara and Castiglione in Urbino. And it was the world of doubt and self-criticism of the Counter-Reformation that was to produce Torquato Tasso. Again, it was the generation that lived through possibly the greatest concentration of political disasters in the history of the peninsula (1500–27) that was to produce Raphael and Leonardo, Michelangelo and Machiavelli; and a world of decadence—the fading greatness of the centuries-old republic of Venice—that produced Carlo Goldoni. Down the centuries Italy has always attracted the foreigner by its extremes and its apparent contrasts, and its literature is as varied and exciting as its history. This heritage, the consciousness of a great literary past, forms part of the experience of every educated Italian today, just as the influence, for example, of classical Rome was felt consistently by Italians, particularly during the Renaissance and the *Risorgimento*.

So if we take our main themes—political conscience, social change, and religion—we shall find them echoing back to the earliest centuries of Italian literature. Themes which have occupied the minds of thinkers and writers, particularly during the last hundred years of Italy's history, and which are still present today have been present in many forms and variations in the Italian literary consciousness from 1300. And from that date—the hypothetical moment when Dante Alighieri started his progress from the dark wood through Hell, Purgatory and Paradise—it is appropriate to survey these themes. At that moment, with a writer of tremendous stature, was born the Italian language as a vehicle for serious literature. In Dante's major work, the *Divine Comedy*, Italy took a great stride out of the dimness of the Dark Ages into a leading position in western culture.

DANTE ALIGHIERI

The world in 1300 was small indeed. Italy was at the centre of a Mediterranean culture just emerging into modern times. The two great contenders for supremacy in the peninsula—the pope and the emperor—had fallen on hard times. The last effective emperor, Conradin, had been decisively defeated by Charles of Anjou in 1268. Boniface VIII, pope from 1294 to 1303, witnessed the collapse of the medieval papacy in Italy and, with it, perhaps the end of the Middle Ages. After a prolonged quarrel with Philip the Fair, of France, Boniface was ignominiously taken prisoner by French troops in 1303 and, after some adventures, was shut up in Rome, powerless to act, where he died in the same year. This act ended a long period in which the popes had represented a significant political force in Europe. Philip engineered the election of a French successor, Clement V (1305–14), who was established at Avignon, under French rather than Italian control, to initiate a series of French puppet popes that was to last for over seventy years.

The final attempt to re-establish the empire in Italy was by Henry VII of Luxemburg, a crusading spirit who crossed the Alps at the head of an army in 1310 in an attempt to impose some sort of order on an Italy torn by strife between factions. The venture was cut short by Henry's death, but the idealism of the enterprise, characterised as 'the last gasp of empire', caught the imagination of Dante, who wrote three famous letters in support of Henry's attempt.

Dante was not simply a chronicler of these events, although most of the main actors find their places in his *Divine Comedy* and his theories on the political state of Italy appear also in his *De Monarchia*. Dante played a significant part in elevating the vernacular—Italian as opposed to Latin—into a literary language. This great task of linguistic selection, of rejection and refining, of elaboration and synthesis found its theoretical expression in his *De Vulgari eloquentia* and its consummation in the *Comedy* itself. Thus, when we read the *Divine Comedy*, we are not only sharing the anguish of the soul in its search for salvation, but participating in the very formative process of a refined currency of expression. The reader who grows impatient with the events of Dante's time, his theology, or even the rigidity of the moral code, cannot escape the power of his poetry.

Dante's *Comedy* stands at the head of Italian literature, its foundation in intellectual and linguistic terms. To understand its background and some of its more polemical and political attitudes, reference must be made to the changes in social and cultural patterns in Italy in the eleventh and twelfth centuries. The emergence of cities is important here. For the main cultural and social centres of Italy were just beginning to emerge as socially and politically cohesive units to challenge the exclusive control of feudal lords from fortified castles. In fact, the growing autonomy of city-states in this period from the claims of the emperor for total control in Italy reached a watershed in 1183 at the Peace of Constance. By this the cities gained the right to organise themselves as states. Economically, a feudal, predominantly land-based society was giving way to a society where trade, commerce and the exchange of money were increasingly more important. With these changes came an increased use of Italian in the everyday affairs of the state.

In brief, this was the world which Dante inherited and which he was to reject in his ideal scheme of things. Of importance for us here is the fact that he was born into the powerful and autonomous state of Florence at a time of growing interest in the Italian tongue. Florence was to exile Dante, instilling in him that note of poignant affection for the city as is experienced by those forced to live far from their place of origin. The fashion for Italian was to produce the *De Vulgari eloquentia* and the momentous decision to write the *Divine Comedy* in something approaching Tuscan, so initiating the long process of refinement and crystallisation of the Italian language in literature.

But there is one further respect in which Dante was a child of his time. His voyage through Hell, Purgatory and Paradise is the search for final truth of one individual soul. The *Comedy* is often referred to as the dramatic analogue of Aquinas' *Summa theologica*, but at root it is the search of one man for himself. In a sense this was the individualisation of an institution, the translation of participation and acquiescence into a personal faith and its intellectual and artistic elaboration. For religion, too, was subject to a new spirit; flagellants and mendicant preachers were everywhere demonstrating a new fervour and new enthusiasm for personal salvation. In short, Dante's works are characterised by political sensibility, religious conscience and a tremendous creative instinct for the language of art, and are worth examining from these points of view.

The language which Dante used for his *Divine Comedy* and elevated to the status of a medium of expression for literature had, of course, sprung from Latin. Before his time there had been two languages in common use: the Latin of classical Rome, for most official purposes and for 'serious' literature, and the *volgare*, derived ultimately from the everyday speech of Rome, for common everyday expression. Just as the Romans used a correct literary language for their greatest literature and a corrupt or debased form in everyday speech, so the Middle Ages adopted the language of Cicero, Virgil, Horace and Livy for literary and official use, and a form corrupted by use for everyday speech. After the fall of the empire and the ensuing barbarian invasions the various regions of Italy developed their own distinct variants of the *volgare*. The rise of cities and the autonomy of the different constituent regions of the peninsula aided this process of fragmentation, and the diversities are still—some hundred years after unification—present in the Italian dialects today.

So the age of Dante began to feel the need to communicate to a wider public in the spoken language. There was already a tradition of literary expression in Italian before the time of Dante. Taking inspiration and forms from the Carolingian and Breton cycles of poems, and utilising the traditions of 'courtly love' poetry in Provence, poetry in the vulgar tongue had become established in Italy before Dante. But its traditions—popular, religious and courtly—lead up to rather than compete with the solid achievement of Dante. The poets of the thirteenth century— the Sicilian School, Guinizelli, Cavalcante and the *Dolce stil novo*— look forward to the love poetry of Dante's *Vita nuova* and their consummation (in linguistic terms) in the *Divine Comedy*.

Dante Alighieri was born in Florence in 1265 into a family of minor noble standing. After a period of study at the University of Bologna, his first excursions into poetry were in the company of his friends Lapo Gianni and Guido Cavalcante. These early poems were collected in his *Vita nuova* and dedicated to a Beatrice —probably Bice, daughter of Folco Portinari and wife of Simone dei Bardi, who died in 1290. To celebrate his love for this girl, Dante collected his poems to her and a commentary in prose into a book which was to become a precursor for the *Comedy*. It represents a crystallisation of poetic currents existing in Italy up to this moment, for such poems as *Ne li occhi porta la mia donna amore* and *Tanto gentile e tanto onesta pare* are a refined and delicate expression of the love of a young man for a lady, and a measure of Dante's early achievement. Love for Beatrice, the exaltation of love as a noble art and a new refinement of poetic expression— these three elements produce the solid value of the poems. They are no longer a game, a device for the expression of love in the relatively rigid system that Dante's contemporaries had adapted from the poetry of courtly love, but an intellectual elaboration of experience and the serious pursuit of the perfection of expression. The indication of this seriousness is already present in the figure of Beatrice. She is far more than the adored but distant object of the poet's love. Rather she is endowed with virtues, having a nobility and gentility calculated to inspire all who meet her, and destined in the *Comedy* to fulfil a high function as an inspiration to Dante and a means to divine grace.

With the figure of Beatrice, therefore, deriving from the stereotyped conventions of courtly-love styles, Dante steps decisively out of the traditions of his forebears and into the world of modern literature, attempting to combine two great preoccupations of literature—the love for woman and the search for God —in one edifice.

After his first excursion into love and poetry in the *Vita nuova*, Dante broadened his experience in life and letters. He wrote other poems of love, destined for another lady and with different stylistic intentions. Two unfinished works—the *Convivio* and the *De*

Vulgari eloquentia—bear on his elaboration of a literary language. In the first section of the *Convivio*—a kind of literary banquet at which the components and ideals of Dante's world are discussed —we find an exaltation of the *volgare*. The spoken tongue is seen as the new light destined to shine in darkness for those who cannot understand Latin, but in the *De Vulgari eloquentia*, the thesis is further elaborated. Dante sees the origins of languages going back to the Tower of Babel; he describes the many dialects spoken by Italians up and down the peninsula and finds no single one of them equal to the task of assuming the burden of literature. Such a language must, in his view, be common to the whole of Italy, be capable of expressing the most elevated subjects and be able to work in the most noble of all metrical forms, the *Canzone*.

So Dante's *Volgare illustre* was to have important characteristics. It was to be *illustre* because the highest and most illustrious tasks would be assigned to it and because it was to be an amalgam of the best—that is to say, the result of a process of stylistic refinement on the part of writers and intellectuals. It was to be *aulico* and *curiale* (from *aula* and *curia*)—that is, pertaining to throne and senate—to be used, therefore, at the seat of government and, finally, *cardinale* (from *cardine*, hinge), as the support and foundation of the Italian language. Dante broke off the work at the fourteenth chapter, and it remained for the *Comedy* to show such a language in action as Dante conceived it.

This was only the beginning of the great debate called the *Questione della lingua*. Writers and linguists down the long course of the history of Italian literature were to debate the appropriateness for literature of the various dialects of the Italian regions, from the theorists and treatise writers of the Renaissance to the work of Alessandro Manzoni in the nineteenth century. Even today, at a short distance historically from the unification of the peninsula, the debate is very much alive in the correspondence columns of newspapers and reviews, and in discussions of the latest dialect-writing.

Before the composition of his theoretical works, among which figures the *De Monarchia*, Dante had begun his political career in Florence and taken the road that was to lead him into exile and provide him with the sources of many of his attitudes to the city. The roots of his political sensibility, then, are to be found in the Florence of his day. The city is also the source of another feature of Dante's work which is of importance to the history of Italian literature: the vital attachment to contemporary political and social events of the *Divine Comedy* itself.

It is arguable that if Dante had not been exiled the *Divine Comedy* would have been different—or might not have been written at all. It is certainly true that the circumstances of his political career had an important effect on the growth of his ideology. He was a committed writer, an author with concrete ideas on the organisation of states, the function of political power, the place of authority and the relative importance of Church and state in the lives of Italians. In a sense, the problems he posed remain unsolved; they strike at the roots of Italian thinking even today, and constitute an early stage in a long tradition of creative writing with a political content or bias. Particularly regarding the role of government and Church, Dante's work is a fascinating insight into medieval Florence and Italy, and his desperate plea for peace in the war-torn world in which he lived is the timeless lament of the intellectual both involved in and detached from the society of his day.

Florence was characterised by internal political struggles of all kinds. The growing professional class, with interests in banking, manufacture and trade, had the advantages of wealth, talent and some political intuition, but were in a minority. The *popolo grasso*, as they were known, were forced to seek alliance with the *popolo minuto* (lower class) or with the nobility. The *popolo grasso* was organised in guilds called *arti maggiori*; the *popolo minuto* into the *arti minori*. The noblemen were the survivors of feudal times; landowners for the most part, their aspirations to political power were often frustrated by lack of leadership and inter-family feuding. The lower class had the advantage of numbers, but tended to waver between a policy of alliance with one or other of the sects and the desire for autonomy of action. In broadest outline, then, a precarious equilibrium existed between the three major divisions of Florentine society; none was powerful enough to prevail on its own and alliances proved unstable. To complicate matters further, within these divisions, at regular intervals, major feuds broke out, such as that of the Cerchi and Donati in 1295, which finally divided the city into the *Bianchi* (Whites) and *Neri* (Blacks). The Whites comprised the Cerchi family with a group of nobles and adherents from other divisions; the Blacks were the Donati, a majority of nobles, and some from the professional class.

This situation of internal rupture was the classic one of political weakness; Florence divided was the opportunity for outside interests. Pope Boniface VIII (whom Dante placed well down in his *Inferno*) saw the chance to further his ambitions to annex Tuscany to the Papal State. He supported the weaker party, the Blacks, since they were more in need of outside help, and sent Charles of Valois with 800 mercenaries to their aid. Thus aided, the Blacks took control of the government, exiling prominent members of the opposition, among whom was Dante Alighieri.

Rather like that of his later compatriot, Machiavelli, Dante's sentence of exile was in some ways the door to literature. Certainly it goes some way to explaining attitudes we find in the *Comedy*. Dante was accused of a number of crimes, condemned to pay a fine and to serve two years' imprisonment, besides being excluded from public office. Following non-payment of the fine, the death sentence was imposed if he should ever enter Florentine territory—and this amounted to banishment. By a tragic irony, therefore, Florence banished her greatest citizen to a life of wandering. Perhaps his sorrow, as well as an early political retirement, released the emotions and created the conditions for the genesis of the *Divine Comedy*.

Dante was, by natural inclination and birth, an aristocrat. He looked back with nostalgia to a smaller Florence, before the coming of riches and a society which seemed to him dominated by the principle of material gain. It would seem natural, therefore, to find him among the nobles, the *Neri*, in support of the Donati faction; but we find him supporting the Cerchi and the *popolo minuto*. For Dante was perhaps too much of a realist and idealist to support the nobility of his own day, of whose faults and short-comings he had had direct experience in political life in Florence. His ideal was that of the *Dolce stil novo*, a nobility of virtue and of spirit, a kind of antique virtue, rather than nobility of birth.

In short, Dante was broadly conservative. He rejected that society that was to produce Petrarch and Boccaccio, looking back to the Middle Ages and to feudalism. From the political confusion of Florence, he supported the values of peace and authority, obedience to central authority and christianity. He stood, too, for the empire as a cohesive political force and against the papacy in its political and temporal ambitions. He was one of the first to divide the spiritual from the temporal power of the papacy, hinting that the territorial ambitions of the pope were a root cause of Florence's—and Italy's—weakness. In this light may be understood the three letters of Dante written in support of the invasion of Italy by the Emperor Henry VII, and in these circumstances can be seen the justification of his theoretical standpoint in the *De Monarchia*. This treatise, written about 1310-12, shows Dante's faith in a strong centralised government as the only hope for divided Italy and faction-ridden Florence. If strength in government resides in a king, then the medieval emperor of the Romans was the obvious and divinely appointed residuum of power. Rome was the fore-ordained centre of government, the home also of the Christian figurehead, the pope. Church and state were to be separate and autonomous authorities, however. In this last principle resides the novelty of the *De Monarchia*, and it was the one which would condemn the book to the flames by 1329 and assure it a place on the Index by 1554.

We have surveyed the themes of Dante's linguistic interests and his political sensibilities; we must now come to his religious conscience and the *Comedy* itself—where all three themes meet and fuse in a poem which is a starting point for Italian literature. Into his greatest work Dante poured the totality of his experience of medieval Italy, but he also chose a framework of absolute harmony. Thus we find, apart from the characters and characteristics of Dante's Florence and the values of contemporary politics, a cornice of divine justice. It is a world of the poet's imagination, but a world which carries the imprint of absolute rightness from the outset. The characters, the sins, the landscape of nightmares and the figures from literature and mythology taken together constitute a totality of vision because subject to a divine order—an order of sins and good works, rewarded by divine wrath or approval. Disappointed by the failure of the emperor's mission and discarded by Florence, Dante set out to describe a world which would not be subject to the laws of petty politics, wars and imperialist popes; all would be subject to the justice of heaven and would be seen in its true light. The *Comedy* is the story not only of Florence and her political difficulties but of entire humanity.

Dante's voyage through Hell, Purgatory and Paradise runs from 8 to 15 April 1300. Having found himself in the dark wood of human sin, and the way forward blocked by the three beasts symbolic of incontinence, violence and fraud—the three obstacles in human experience to the soul's consciousness of sin—Dante is guided by the Latin poet Virgil to find the path towards this consciousness. As Dante is helped by Virgil, so the soul is aided by the power of human reason: 'humanity supported by philosophic reason and guided by imperial authority towards the earthly paradise'. It was Beatrice, the object of Dante's love in the *Vita nuova*, who had despatched Virgil to Dante's aid. And Beatrice has come to symbolise theology, or humanity inspired by the Revela-

tion of God and directed by the Church to lead the soul towards
the glory of Heaven. Dante is guided by Virgil down through the
vast cone of Hell, pausing to note the sins and sinners in their
progessive degradation. Having traversed nine circles, he reaches
the centre where Lucifer, the fallen angel, represents the full
horror of sin personified. Having lived through the consciousness
of sin in all its horrible forms, the soul begins the slow ascent of
Purgatory, a mountain imagined rising from the sea, divided
again into nine sections of progressive revelation, until he reaches
the earthly Paradise, with its nine heavens, and the Empyrean.
Into this graphic representation of every gradation of moral experience—from utter damnation to beatitude—Dante places the
population of his age, his past and literary heritage, each judged,
then condemned or lifted up according to his deserts.

The structure of Dante's justice is relatively simple: punishment
is regulated by *contrappasso*, where each soul is subjected to a
form of the sin he perpetrated on earth, or by analogy, where a
poetic justice is meted out by God. The *Comedy* is far from simply
a catalogue of errors, however, as each new personage strikes a
chord in the mind of Dante's reader, and, in the *Inferno* above all,
lives a 'life' of incident supported by the full range of a consummate imagination and supreme artistry. The lovers, Paolo and
Francesca, the heroic Ulysses, Farinata degli Uberti, Brunetto
Latini, Pier della Vigna and the father of Dante's friend, Guido
Cavalcante, are all invested with the full clothing of the lives
they lived on earth, are caught, suspended, as it were, *in flagrante
delicto*, in moments which sum up the totality of their position in
Dante's system of retribution and reward. To err is human, and
the humanity and pathos of Dante's characters survive even the
terrible lesson they are intended to preach, to become literary
masterpieces of giant proportions.

Thus it is that the reader of Canto V of the *Inferno* will hear the
tale of Paolo and Francesca in all the delicate colours of the *Dolce
stil novo*, that school of the poetry of love to which Dante

belonged in his youth, and will forget their sin for he shares Dante's compassion and may be moved to pity as much as his guide. The reader may be moved similarly by the awful fate of Ugolino, condemned with his sons to death in the tower; he may follow the description of Farinata, whom even hell could never completely tame, painted with vigour and realism in the colours of his life on earth, or he may be drawn to Cavalcante, who with dignity and resignation inquires of Dante the whereabouts of his son. The power of attraction resides in the figure of Dante himself. We do not see the fiery pit of hell solely through the eyes of Dante the author—to avert our gaze when the sight is unbearable—but we see also Dante the character, his relationship with Virgil, his love for Beatrice and all his reactions. From this there is no escape. Dante's compassion, his horror, his righteous anger and his fainting may be the reactions of the reader. We ourselves are drawn into the experience of the poet by this vital link—Dante's humanity, just as the human soul, in its full consciousness of sin, may aspire to purgation and ultimately redemption.

So the modern reader may wonder about a divorce of Dante's purpose and his achievement. He may be tempted to separate the 'picturesque horrors' of the *Inferno* from their vital positioning in Dante's supreme structure—rather as a reader with a taste for graphic art might leaf through Doré's massive volume of illustrations to the *Comedy* without digesting the poem. A balanced approach to the *whole* poem rights the balance, however, and repays the effort, for Dante is consistent with his chosen framework. The horror of sin in the *Inferno* gives way in the *Purgatorio* to the calm of repentance and to the joy of Heaven in the *Paradiso*. The craggy landscape of the *Inferno* yields to a more abstract, ethereal context, as the essentially earthly reality of sin recedes gradually from view to be replaced by biblical characters and the discussion of heavenly love. The balance of justice is sustained, and in pure literary terms we find characters who seem less moulded, less compelling, for they are no longer subject to the full range of human passion. Virgil, the 'virtuous pagan', hands over to Beatrice when he can logically go no farther, for Dante is now to be guided by the Church's teachings and the Holy Spirit. Dante must purify himself before proceeding, must undergo examination—and be found human—before contemplating the face of Beatrice and the fullness of divine grace. Thus purged and qualified, the soul may ascend the nine strata of Paradise through the examples of virtue ranged about him, and through the growing brilliance of divine light, until he looks upon the face of God.

This, then, is the soul's journey, a monument to the literary elaboration of the drama of good and evil in every man. But Dante's *Comedy* was not simply the supreme statement of the Catholic conscience. It was also a formula for political action for his day: '*storica, politica, militante*', in the words of one 'committed' critic.[1] For the poem is a synthesis of the universal and the personal—universal in the struggle of the human conscience between human passions and divine justice; personal in that it is peopled by Dante's own friends and enemies—and contains political concepts appropriate to his own ideology. This may be seen in part in the *Convivio*, the *De Monarchia* and in Dante's letters. Even in the *Comedy* we find constant echoes of the poet's hopes for Florence, Italy and himself. Inserted with masterly precision into Dante's structure of vice and virtue, and supported by what we have called Dante's humanity, these echoes are universalised to become, in a sense, inevitable, a commentary on man's political state in all times.

Dante's political campaign, if such it can be called, surfaces in many places. Brunetto Latini, who is seen by one tradition as Dante's teacher, prophesies his exile; Dante's ancestor, Cacciaguida, urges Dante to broadcast the virtues of peace and justice to the world, in the *Paradiso*; Ciacco harshly criticises the decadent state of Florence. Dante himself in his conversation with Pope Nicholas III berates the Church for its vice and corruption. Again, in the conversation with Virgil and Sordello in the

Purgatorio, Italy appears as a ship without a helmsman, and even the women of Florence come under the whiplash of his invective in the mouth of Forese Donati. In many places Dante's passion for justice and his profound feeling for the state of Florence are apparent. They are seen consistently against the background of an image: the pope and the emperor in their rightful autonomous positions in harmony with an Italy at peace.

FRANCESCO PETRARCA

If Dante had given Italy the greatest monument to her moral and religious conscience, Petrarch gave her an unequalled primacy in the European love lyric. Although Petrarch was seventeen when Dante died in 1321, the two poets represent complementary facets of medieval Italian culture. In a sense, Dante's gigantic vision of justice under authoritative secular and religious powers—man in his rightful place within fixed systems—gives way to Petrarch's view of man at war with himself. Dante's poetic vision looked back to the Italy of pope and emperor and patched up that world in his imagination to create an ideal system by the standards of the thirteenth century. Petrarch was firmly rooted in the fourteenth century and set Italian literature securely on the path to the Renaissance.

Generalisations about 'new' and 'old' worlds need some elaboration, however, as it so often seems that more than a generation separates the two poets. In the fourteenth century, Italian society suffered a period of crisis and some severe setbacks whose echoes appear to be reflected in the writings of prominent intellectuals, like Petrarch. The crisis of his conscience, his almost continuous uncertainty about the values of his age, is in some ways the crisis of his century.

Dante had moved in a world where the twin authorities of Church and empire were recent enough to be remembered. The decline of these two institutions—the pope reduced to a French puppet in Avignon and the emperor eclipsed in political terms by the rise of national identity and independence—had given way in the *trecento* to a new and fast-developing society. The development of trade and the expansion of markets produced an economy in the major Italian cities which looks forward to capitalism. The ancient corporations, or trade associations, began to be replaced by powerful groups with greater financial power. All over Europe life was changing fast; the loyalties of feudal knights in war were giving way to hired mercenaries in the control of *condottieri*; new social structures were emerging and, in Europe in general, society was moving towards the creation of the national state, with the monarch at its head.

But in Italy the process of crystallisation into nationhood stopped halfway; the weakening of both papacy and empire left rival factions which became the *signorie*. Florence, Milan, Venice and Naples led the field in importance, with a host of minor states existing by virtue of the protection of one or more of these city-states. This was the political landscape which was to find its most colourful expression culturally in the Renaissance, but, in the fourteenth century, had all the uncertainty and relative insecurity of novelty. This is the background to the figure of Petrarch. If Dante was to retire from the world of active politics in the sense that he took refuge in the unassailable retreat of divine justice, Petrarch's writing shows him a child of his age, living in it and suffering by it intellectually throughout his life. For the anguish of his moral, political and religious conscience fills his works and provides an ever-changing rhythm of conflicts and tensions. While Dante found, in a poetic sense at least, a formula, a solution and, in it, peace, Petrarch represents to the last poem in the *Canzoniere* the doubts and wonderings of Everyman.

This does not mean that Petrarch is any less important to the evolution of Italian literature and to our present themes. For he looks forward to the fifteenth and sixteenth centuries in his intellectual achievements and his preoccupation with the place of man in the universe. The fifteenth century was to follow his example of study and emulation of the great Latin writers and transmit the lesson of humanism to the sixteenth century. The sixteenth century was to adopt his poetic forms and images—along with his entire theory of love—imitating every aspect of his poetic achievement in a process that continues into modern times. Finally, Petrarch dramatised the struggles of an individual conscience in such a way as to make them universal. And this last factor, a kind of 'consciousness of self', an intellectualisation of sentiment and a species of high seriousness, has echoes far beyond the Renaissance, into Romanticism, even perhaps to the nineteenth-century preoccupation with the inner self. For art in general, certainly, the principle of balance between emotional inspiration and intellectual elaboration—a synthesis which Petrarch brought to a pitch of excellence—was to have a long run in the literature of the Italians.

Francesco Petrarca was born on 20 July 1304 at Arezzo into a family which, like Dante, had been exiled from Florence originally. He studied at Carpentras, Montpellier and Bologna, where he took a degree in law. On 6 April 1327 he saw Laura in a church at Avignon, and his love for her became one of the great events of literature. The origins of Laura are obscure, although the subject is not without its theorists, and her very existence has been doubted. She lives most tangibly, however, as the central myth of Petrarch's *Canzoniere*, his book of lyric poems, where—more an inspiration or excuse for self-examination than a real person—she mirrors the poet's aspirations, his ideology of love, and above all his inner conflicts. Having finished the studies which had qualified him to practise law, he abandoned all ambitions of a legal nature and moved in the circle of the powerful Colonna family, entering the service, finally, of Cardinal Giovanni Colonna. From this point in 1330, Petrarch's life was one of continual travelling, satisfying his thirst for new experiences, until he came to rest at Valchiusa.

In 1341 he was crowned as a poet of universally recognised stature in Rome at a ceremony which represented for him the height of achievement on earth. But in the following year there began a period of intense disquiet for Petrarch; the period 1342–50 saw not only the death of his brother, but the adventure of Cola di Rienzo (see below) and the death of Laura along with many of Petrarch's friends in the great plague of 1348. In this period, he wandered restlessly, living in Milan, Venice and Paris, until he moved to Venice in 1361, where he lived for seven years as a guest of the Venetian senate. Finally he moved to Padua, and then to Arquà in the Euganean hills, where he died in 1374.

In a way similar to, though also radically different from the work of Dante, Petrarch's writing reflects those great themes which we are suggesting are characteristic of Italian literature: political sensibility, moral and religious conscience and linguistic innovation. With Dante in mind we shall find some similarities in considering Petrarch's political life, for he, too, had his champion. Henry VII had disappointed Dante in his hopes for the restitution of a central authority at the helm of government. Petrarch's champion, Cola di Rienzo, was also to fail, and leave the poet with a similar taste of human weakness. Cola's plan was basically the restoration of the liberty of republican Rome, the collection of all the Italian states into a free and loose federation in order to restore the Italian peninsula to its former pre-eminence in Europe. Petrarch's enthusiasm for Cola di Rienzo and his designs emerges clearly from his letters, and here, too, we find his political ideology. Not now the principle of rightful and just authority, as in Dante, but the spirit of liberty. This liberty was to have been the autonomy of the Italian *signorie* from outside interference, and the cessation of internal struggles between them in an atmosphere of peace and co-operation. Without the machinations of pope and emperor, the states might coalesce in a spirit of mutual trust, even if they did not unite. But Petrarch was hardly a precursor in the struggle for Italian unity, for he was a poet and scholar before he was a politician. Central to his dream for the peninsula was the image of Rome, as always, a rebirth of the political and historical greatness of the republic—not, it should be noted, in this case, the seat of empire and papacy, but the scholar's yearning for the civic values of a bygone age. However far such a plan may have been from the practical realities of Petrarch's day, its descendant, the science of humanism, was to have an immense effect on the generations to follow.

In what lies the modernity of Petrarch's political attitudes? A new sense of liberty, perhaps. Reproached on a number of occasions for the apparent inconsistencies of his various profitable, but transitory, allegiances with tyrannical rulers, Petrarch stated his freedom to devote himself to study and contemplation under the aegis of whoever was prepared to support and further these activities. So liberty in politics must also be liberty from politics. Intellectual pursuits began to acquire with Petrarch a value for themselves and the dignity of some autonomy from traditional loyalties. For Petrarch was also modern in his freedom from close identification with any one of the Italian states, becoming, in his incessant travelling, almost an example of that free association of states under Rome of which he had dreamed, almost more 'Italian' than many who bear the name today. Modern, above all, was Petrarch's love for Italy and celebration of her as superior to other nations. For in this last sentiment all the various and apparently conflicting ideals of his writing find their union: his promotion of a monarchy in the person of Robert of Anjou, as the force most likely to unify the efforts of all Italians; his support for a return of the pope to Rome from Avignon, so that that city might rise up again from its present squalor, and his celebration, above all, perhaps, of the beauties of the Italian natural scene, the setting for all his work and the landscape of his love for Laura.

Modern, too, and yet in keeping with the spiritual revival of the Catholic religion in the age of Dante, was Petrarch's attitude to the Church. And this brings us to the theme of moral and religious conscience. He was critical in all his writings of the corruption of the clergy and the curia, but remained faithful to the idea of the pope returned to his rightful position in Rome. We find his invective against corrupt practices, together with the idea of a great reformer who was to come to purify the institution, in the *sonetti antiavignonesi* as well as in his letters *sine nomen*.[2]

But it is the group of political *Canzoni* with, at their head, the famous *Italia mia* (CXXVIII) that carry the full force of Petrarch's campaign. They show Petrarch feeling deeply for the misfortunes of Italy and committed (in a scholarly and poetic sense) to save her from ruin. *Italia mia* was a *canzone* much remembered in the nineteenth century and at other moments of heightened national consciousness. It depicts a somewhat utopian Italy, free from internal strife, free from the devastating incursions of foreign mercenary soldiers, elevated to a new pride in herself and freed from foreign domination. No less important in this respect is the well-known *canzone Spirito gentil* (LVII), an exhortation to action, although we do not know to whom it was directed. Rome emerges again here, raised to its antique prestige and glory, and to peace and order, to become the kingpin of Petrarch's political philosophy. The contrast in the poem between the good order of classical Rome and its chaotic state in the Middle Ages recalls to the modern reader Leopardi's *Ginestra* (see p 63), where Rome is contrasted with another age. It is a concept which will give life and breadth to the Renaissance, but remains the politics of the scholar and idealist. To take another example: in sonnet XXVIII Petrarch campaigns vigorously for a crusade against the infidel Turk, but the classical echoes in the poem, the re-evocation of the struggle between Greeks and Turks, remind us that the poem is the intellectual elaboration of an ideal. Just as in his Latin epic, the *Africa*, ideals and hopes for a modern Christianity mingle with the echoes of a past greatness, so the poem is also rooted essentially in the process of literary and intellectual elaboration.

It may seem strange to see the main body of Petrarch's Italian poems to Laura as illustrative of moral and religious conscience, but this is in fact what they are. The poems in celebration of Petrarch's love for Laura represent the greatest refinement of the individual moral conscience in Italian literature, and look forward to modern times in their capacity for self-examination. For Petrarch raised Laura to the function of an ideal, and so dismissed her from personal participation in his *Canzoniere*. This is not to say that she is unimportant; rather she appears in many guises as the object of his love, invested with those physical and moral characteristics that have become universal. But she is always a presence just out of reach, never quite able to descend from the pedestal of perfection, for the poems are really about the poet himself. Petrarch examines his own conscience and finds his love for Laura a distraction from the pursuit of divine love; he discovers his desire for earthly glory in conflict with his conviction that the things of this life are transitory and insubstantial. Taken as extreme positions, these are the poles between which his restless and anguished spirit moves in many of his poems, and this deep-felt internal struggle is a source of their energy. The key to this struggle, known in Italian as Petrarch's *dissidio*, is in his *Secretum*, or secret. And here the catharsis of the *Canzoniere* finds its complement in a dialogue in three books between Petrarch and St Augustine. In a pitiless self-examination Petrarch uncovers the full range of his doubts and conflicts, and provides the full exposition in prose of his emotional states, in the *Canzoniere*.

What, then, is Petrarch's *Canzoniere*? On the surface, 366 poems of love for Laura in life, in death, with a few devoted to sacred and other subjects. The first poem, *Voi ch'ascoltate in rime sparse il suono*, poses the moral problem and introduces the struggle. Petrarch confesses that his course in life has been a mistaken one, that his sighs of love, his *vario stile*, vain hopes and vain sorrows have been to no point. Both his love for Laura and his yearning for glory in critical approval for his works have brought him nothing but repentance and the full knowledge that *quanto piace al mondo è breve sogno* (all that is pleasing to the world is a brief dream). This poem, traditionally regarded as the manifesto and written or finished late in the genesis of the book, gives the key to the introspection of the poet, his wavering allegiances to life's preoccupations, exaltation and joy matched always by despair and repentance, but also establishes the poetic tone of the *Canzoniere*. This is meditative and balanced, calm and thoughtful—in short, an expression of deeply felt emotion through the medium of an exacting literary form.

These considerations may be observed in all the poems to Laura. Indeed, Petrarch's mastery of the sonnet and *canzone* forms has sometimes given rise to impatience in generations born since the onset of romanticism who demand 'spontaneity' or 'immediacy' from poetry. But this is to misunderstand the fourteenth century fundamentally. For such is the refinement of language and the carefully balanced rhythm of images, from octave to sestet, and even within the tightness of a single poetic line, that Petrarch often conveys an impression both of directness of felt emotion and artistry of expression. And here lies another key to the importance of Petrarch: the crystallisation into a model for all to use—and abuse—of the sonnet form.

So perhaps this was Petrarch's third great contribution to the Italian literary heritage: the language and forms of the European love lyric. With him it is no longer appropriate to talk of *schools* of poetry in Italy, as in the age of Dante. The *Canzoniere* is a great single statement of poetic form whose impact on later generations is comparable with that of the language of Dante. Petrarch was not concerned, as Dante had been, with the forms of words and regional variants, being less 'Florentine' in this respect, but rather gave to Italian literature the rhythms of lyric poetry, the discipline and structure of the poetic statement within prescribed limits.

When reading a Petrarchan sonnet it is sometimes difficult to associate the author with the world of Dante, with his 'medieval imaginings', with the *signorie* and the disordered and chaotic state of medieval Italy. The unity of the poet's vision, his statelessness in Italian terms, and his probing into the conflicts in the human conscience mark him as a modern soul in torment, a man at sea, so to speak, tossed by the storms of his own passions and tortured by his moral convictions. It is Petrarch, then, more than Dante, who points the way ahead to our own uncertainties, and fore-shadows the modern literary history of the Italians.

GIOVANNI BOCCACCIO

With Boccaccio we come to the third great exponent of literature in medieval Italy and to a figure who complements the literary personalities of Dante and Petrarch. For to Dante's vision of the human moral conscience and Petrarch's probing into that conscience at war with itself, we must now add Boccaccio's 'realism', his mirror of fourteenth-century Italian society, the *human comedy* of that age. With him, we shall move far from the world of divine justice or the refinement of the love lyric—into the world of narrative, in fact, and with the *Decameron*, we shall arrive at the short-story form.

Our first task is to define more closely the kind of short story that Boccaccio perfected and collected into his version of the 'Arabian Nights'. It is essential, for instance, to separate him from that critical tradition which used to see him as a popular teller of vulgar tales, the fabricator of a kind of comic travesty of the serious world of Dante and Petrarch. Such misapprehensions were the result of the attempt to impose on his *Decameron* the values of an age which was not Boccaccio's, and were sustained by the long-standing popularity of the work in translations, truncated and expurgated editions and ill-conceived digests, intended primarily for an uncritical market. The truth of Boccaccio's achievement is far from this; rather the prose tradition, that bore its most precious fruit in the *Decameron*, brought Boccaccio—like

Dante and Petrarch—out of the realm of the exclusively popular and provincial, and into an artistic statement of enduring validity. Like his co-founders of the Italian literary heritage, Boccaccio translated a popular and predominantly oral tradition into a literary form of solidity and vitality.

Nor is the image of the mirror of medieval society sufficient definition for Boccaccio's greatest work, for the *Decameron* is the result of a unique and personal vision. It is a betrayal of this individuality to see the *novelle* simply as a kaleidoscope of Italian life, a kind of merry-go-round of characters and popular situations invested with a humorous and artificial context. Boccaccio's vision is a personal statement of freedom; unbound by the strictures of a moral or religious ideology, the author's fantasy may wander at will across a vast terrain of human experience, pausing when the mood takes him to illustrate one or more facets of human experience—allowing the good to lose sometimes, a virtuous husband to be betrayed or a nun to fall in love. Built on the tradition of storytelling in Italian literary history, the *Decameron* lifts that tradition into the realm of art. Basically, the work is a celebration of the essentially human and fundamentally serious quality of intelligence—intelligence understood as astuteness, shrewdness and the ability to gain the advantage over one's fellows—for Boccaccio, *Ingegno*. Beside intelligence stands another medieval abstraction, fortune, or *Fortuna*, against whose cruel dictates or happy situations the intelligence of man is pitted. And finally the context of the struggle is so often the battleground of love, *Amore*. So the *Decameron* is a comedy of adventures and confrontations between these medieval abstractions, a triumph of individual wit and intelligence. But a glance at Boccaccio's framework will remind us of the comprehensive quality of his intention, his 'medieval' cornice, and will point too to his limitations. For the *Decameron* has often been seen as complementary to the *Divine Comedy—commedia umana* to *divina commedia*, in the words of De Sanctis—and it is a generalisation that still holds good of the design and spirit of the work. It should not lead us into an assessment of the *Decameron* which places it on a level with Dante's masterpiece, however, for this would exaggerate its importance.

Boccaccio's *Decameron* is the other side of the coin as far as the Italian literary heritage is concerned. No longer can we define, as with Dante and Petrarch, a specific ideology and political and religious standpoint. With Boccaccio we have the *human comedy*: the attempt to express the many tones and gradations of a society according to a loosely defined but given formula, to depict human activity from its lowest to its highest aspirations, and therefore to exclude a specific moral or religious standpoint. Further, such standpoints, if we could deduce them from accurate biographical documentation, would represent the author and not his work, or would represent the work as polemical in ways that it is not. The *Decameron* is, therefore, the artistic expression of medieval Italian life on a broad canvas—a work which brings to mind (in the dimensions of its intention) the *Comédie Humaine* of Balzac or the novel cycle of Verga (see p 108).

Such a comparison may cause surprise. What, it may be asked, has Boccaccio's earthy realism to do with the naturalism, or *verismo*, of the nineteenth century? But the comparison serves to underline the validity and seriousness of Boccaccio's intention within the limitations imposed on him by his age. Of course, we are not suggesting for Boccaccio a 'programme' of the kind proposed by nineteenth-century novelists, but rather that his vision of his society, his search for truth and his choice of a carefully designed structure are consistent with a similar spirit and intention. If the nineteenth century was to 'calibrate' human experience against a scale of social values, this was because those values were the currency of that age. Boccaccio's world was the fourteenth century and its immediate past. Not the Paris salon, then, nor the peasant economy of Sicily, but a society in which a commonly accepted framework would be the activities of man measured against the great abstractions of fortune, love and intelligence, and seen against a shifting backcloth of a church grown venal and secular in its officers and practices, or a society coming to be dominated by the forces of trade and commerce. Hence, as we shall see, a majority of the *novelle* are concerned with love—a free commodity, outside civil and religious institutions, to be won or lost by intrigue, luck and intelligence—and the predominance in setting and characters of, respectively, the merchants' world of cut and thrust, reflecting Boccaccio's own experience of Naples, and the imperfections and humanity of those in holy orders.

Giovanni Boccaccio was born about 1313, almost certainly at Certaldo, and grew up in an atmosphere of commerce and trade. Much has been made of this formative influence, and it is true that the Neapolitan commercial background provides some of the brightest colours of the *Decameron*. He was sent by his father to Naples on business, and remained there until 1340, studying and gaining experience of life at the court of King Robert of Anjou. In his early years, it seems that he was mostly self-taught, abandoning the study of law for letters. Having returned to Florence, he spent the greater part of his life in the city, leaving it only to undertake various missions to other parts of Italy for his compatriots. The most important events of these years were perhaps Boccaccio's meeting with Petrarch in 1350 and their subsequent friendship, and a religious crisis which overtook him in 1362. He received news of a prophecy which foretold an early death unless he abandoned the pursuit of poetry. This uneasy state of mind, a phenomenon which we have seen endemic to the conscience of Petrarch himself, was not untypical of the years of spiritual crisis in which the two poets lived. And it was Petrarch who persuaded Boccaccio not to burn his writings. After thirteen more years in which Boccaccio suffered illness and financial difficulties, he died in 1375, the year after Petrarch, and brought to a close the century in which the foundations of the Italian literary heritage were laid.

The outward structure of the *Decameron* may be described fairly simply. Its point of departure is the great plague of 1348. A horrific account of this pestilence is at once balanced by a description of the idyllic calm of a country villa, where a company of young people have taken refuge. Refuge from the turmoil of city life becomes also a refuge from infection. Thus in his opening Boccaccio fixed points of reference in time and place and provided a setting detached from the realities of everyday life for his exploration of those realities. In fact, the group of young men and women, now safe from the ravages of plague in the city, each sets out to relate a short story a day, over a period of ten days. And in the atmosphere of pleasurable escape from the grim reality of death we have almost a symbolic divide between *Divina commedia* and *commedia umana*. The life of Dante's comedy was a preparation for death and beyond; whereas the comedy of Boccaccio celebrates this life on earth in all its vivid colours and transitory, momentary pleasures.

Like all writers who have attempted to describe the 'comedy' of human experience, Boccaccio classifies experience. For Dante the soul's itinerary was from self-knowledge through purgation to joy; Boccaccio's itinerary, on the other hand, is the experiment of man who pits his wits against his destiny from day to day. In the 'comedy of man', the circles are not those of sins and virtues, but are instead the stages in the struggle with *Fortuna*, *Amore* and *Ingegno*. On the first day, we find a condemnation of vice in great men; on the second, the tales depict man at the mercy of fortune; on the third, he is able to overcome fortune by his own ingenuity. The fourth and fifth days are given over to love, its power being shown by a representation of the joy and sorrow it may bring. There follow the tales of man's struggle with his fellow men and the urge to overcome and win, through his native wit and intelligence. This urge is seen in verbal exchanges on the sixth day, and through deception and intrigue in love on the seventh and eighth days. On the ninth day, the narrators pause to take up again the various themes already illustrated, before the finale of the tenth day which balances, with true medieval symmetry, the initial campaign against human vice. For the final day seems to build on the foundations already laid, to represent virtue as the prime qualification for true nobility, seen in terms of fortune (*novelle* 1–3), love (*novelle* 4–7), and intelligence (*novelle* 8–9). The last *novella* shows these three forces in combination—overcome by virtue.

The scheme has all the balance and logic of a medieval system, and was far from new when Boccaccio used it. In artistic terms, it is also far from the whole story, being merely the growth point, or skeleton, which Boccaccio filled with the life of his imagination and creative adaptations of the popular tales of his day. The structure itself is only dimly discerned. With Dante the moral framework is present explicitly or implicitly in every line of the *Comedy*, to give it force and coherence and a rock-like purpose. With Boccaccio it is the excuse for a riot. One of the factors which remains perennially fascinating to the modern reader is the extent to which Boccaccio caught so many of the attitudes and characteristics of that society in transition—from the rigidity of a world of chivalrous traditions and feudal loyalties to a society peopled by the new heroes of trade and exploration.

But that world and its heroes underwent a very particular stylistic treatment in the *Decameron*, and this brings us to the unity of the work. For the secret which ties the whole bundle of tales into a whole is not the narrators and their situation, nor is it any metaphysical formula we may like to impose on it. It is rather Boccaccio's realism, the successful attempt to make even the most absurd situations seem real, and the ability to create the impression that he paints from life. This factor again distances Boccaccio from the other great founders of the Italian literary heritage, Dante and Petrarch, and separates him from ideologies. It is the imagination of the author and his observation of life around him that provides the motive force of the work, rather than any hypothetical progress towards the triumph of virtue. Thus we have a full range of motives current in Boccaccio's day, and even if we notice elements that are particularly his—the vivacity of the commercial scene, the huge number of examples of the fool vanquished in love by the astute, and a not quite balanced invective against the practices of officers of the Church—the harmony of the whole derives ultimately from this realism. In some ways, paradoxically, this realism was a flight from reality, for the 'calibration of experience', that we have suggested is typical of the 'comedy' genre, is in the end the work of fancy or whim. In this Boccaccio's attitude, his standpoint in the tales, may wander at will, as he is free from the strictures of the kind of moral system that bound Dante. This may give rise to the accusation of superficiality. But, in spite of its freedom, its cruelty, occasional malice and frequent obscenity, the *Decameron* is unified by a vision of life which combines acute observation of life as it is and considerable psychological penetration. The work is tied securely to concrete realities fixed firmly in time and place.

It has become fashionable to stress the medieval quality of the *Decameron*, rooted as it is in the oral and poetic 'popular' tradition. It also provides fertile soil for source hunters, and indeed the analysis of one of Boccaccio's tales alongside its forebears gives revealing information about his stylistic and moral intentions; but, date and sources apart, it is the artistic whole which strikes the reader in the present. The irony, the humour and the endless variety of incidents celebrating the human quality of intelligence are the qualities which compel. They are also qualities which foreshadow later chapters in the story of Italian literature, particularly, perhaps, Machiavelli.

Thus the Italian literary heritage was the work of three men in its most important and significant aspects, and the production of the first three-quarters of the fourteenth century. Already we have seen some of the major themes of Italian literature, themes which will recur in the writing of the Italians, expressing that spirit which is endemic to the people and tied to the fortunes of the peninsula. The Italy of the present and recent past has not forgotten its heritage. The unity of the peninsula has not obscured the separateness of the various Italian regions. The predominance of Tuscan forms in the literary language has not hidden the dialect inflections of almost all Italians at home. The idea of Rome as the source of antique glory, the origin of political greatness and the seat of Christendom is reflected in its present position as the seat of government, the home of the papacy, and now the hinge, so to speak, between the two faces of present-day Italian civilisation: north and south. This very division, a serious problem still, where deployment of economic resources and the balance of agricultural and industrial development are concerned, reflects, in a sense, the old division between the kingdoms of Naples, and later of the Two Sicilies, and the northern states.

Before examining the modern literature of the Italians, it has seemed appropriate to look back. In doing so, we have not attempted to describe all the works—or even all the aspects—of the founders of Italian literature, but rather to point to those factors which have endured in the Italian literary consciousness, those aspects which were to find other expressions and other contexts in the Italy of our more recent acquaintance. In Dante and Petrarch we found political and religious sensibilities that already look forward to the great problems of Italian literature in modern times—in Dante, particularly, the sense of *patria*, the bonds of sentiment with a particular regional culture and system; with Petrarch, a kind of 'statelessness', but a feeling for the fortunes of Italy that runs deep, balanced again, as it were, by Dante's creation of a literary language from the *volgare*, a thing that was to become Italian in the infinite variety of subsequent literature. In Petrarch, too, we found the literature of the individual conscience, a portent for all romanticism, consummate scholarship, the door to the Renaissance and, in his forms and poetic metres, a concrete model for the future of the European love lyric. In a lesser key, perhaps, Boccaccio looks forward to the Italian narrative tradition in the human comedy. Less universal in his expression of the values of the 'waning of the Middle Ages', he nevertheless provides the leavening influence of humour and *a priori* realism, to balance the high seriousness of Dante and Petrarch. He looked at men as they were rather than as they might have been, and gave to Italian literature a start in those streams of literature whose preoccupations have been realist, naturalist or, for Italy, *verist*.

The literature of modern Italy, as we shall now see, is amply illustrative of these themes, reflecting in a broad historical sweep, fundamental historical, political and social preoccupations. It is now appropriate to examine them individually, against the background of the societies in which they prospered.

Notes to this chapter are on p 175.

CHAPTER 2

The Political Conscience

For the purposes of this chapter, three 'moments' in the history of the Italians have been chosen. This does not mean that the political conscience is absent from other periods, but rather that a consciousness of political realities provides a *dominant* theme at those moments. It means also that there have been moments in Italian history when the tensions of national life in the peninsula produced a *heightened* consciousness of political tensions, and that this process is reflected in the political context of works of literature.

The background to this process of translation into art of a particular kind of experience has its roots in historical characteristics we have touched on already. In some respects, this may be simplified as the principles of separateness and unity in the history of the Italian people. Thus, in the Renaissance, Machiavelli could propose a loose federation of Italian states under a Florentine ruler when he believed that peace and freedom from foreign domination in Italy might result from such a political formula.[1] For him, however, this was hardly a statement of *Italianità*, but rather a political expedient which aimed to secure stability for Florence—and it goes no further. In the nineteenth century, aspirations towards the unity of the peninsula under one flag were still largely motivated by local and regional requirements, and freedom from the oppression of the foreigner loomed large

again, particularly in Sicily and Lombardy. In the twentieth
century the situation is more complex, for we must consider the
literature of resistance (with a small 'r') to Fascism before World
War II as well as that of the Resistance movement during it. But
here again nationalist sentiments were motivated in part by a
desire to rid the country of the foreign occupier, and the sense of
unity was perhaps more poignant after 1943 with the division of
Italy into two camps.

Crisis and disaster, invasion and occupation—these were the
stark realities of Italy's most tragic and colourful historical
moments. As in all societies, patriotism and identification with a
cause, the individual experience of heroism and self-sacrifice, and
speculation about political systems themselves, thrive in such
conditions. In the modern history of the Italians, therefore, the
moments of heightened political and national consciousness have
been those of national disaster. And those moments, for a
thousand years and more, have been inextricably linked with the
invasion or occupation of the peninsula by the foreigner. Renaissance, *Risorgimento* and Resistance are convenient labels to describe the three great political traumas of the Italian people in
modern times—traumas because their national life was over-
turned. Irreversible changes in ways of living and habits of
thought took place, and, importantly, literature acquired a political 'colour', reflecting the sacrifices of patriotism, the necessity of
release from tragedy in writing and the concomitant speculation
about politics itself.

In a sense, the phrase 'politics itself' brings us naturally to
Machiavelli. For he was responsible, more than any other
Italian, for the concept of politics as a self-sufficient science. But
it should not be forgotten that there are different ways in which
politics and literature can meet. A work may deal with politics
itself; it may describe in a serious and scientific way a political
problem, or propose a political solution, as in Machiavelli's *Il
Principe* or Alfieri's *Della Tirannide*. And here it must stand as a

valid meditation on the human condition if it is not to become a pamphlet or recruiting poster. Or it may reflect political ideas or a political situation, as in the political novels of the nineteenth and twentieth centuries—works by Stendhal and Dostoevsky, for instance, or Malraux and Silone. But a further distinction needs to be made. Italian literature of a truly 'political' conscience is that in which the political idea or situation is itself, in some way, the subject of the work, or central to it. This is literature which has its distinguished ancestry in Dante's *De Monarchia*, or in Petrarch's *All'Italia*, perhaps. On the other hand, literature which arises from the results of political events, embodying a social consciousness rather than a political conscience, we have called the literature of social change. This latter category, whose ancestry is perhaps closer to Boccaccio's *Decameron* in the broader canvas of the human comedy, and which finds its natural outlet in the novel form, will contitute the next chapter.[2]

NICCOLÒ MACHIAVELLI

Niccolò Machiavelli was born in Florence in 1469 and died in 1527. His lifespan represents one of the most turbulent periods in the history of Italy. In the loss by the Italian city states of their independence to the foreign invader, the period saw one of the most radical changes in the life of the peninsula in modern times. Like Dante, a forced retirement from active political life led him to meditate on these tumultuous changes, and resulted in the most influential political writing in Italian history. Machiavelli's *Il Principe* and his *Discorsi sopra la prima deca di Tito Livio* were a direct result of his experience of these events.

Before the eventful years of Machiavelli's maturity, politics was a domestic game played between the five major powers in the peninsula: the papacy, Milan, Naples, Florence and Venice. In a time of prosperity and economic expansion, a kind of political equilibrium had been reached in the fourteenth and fifteenth centuries; inter-state rivalries and conflicts of interest were often settled locally in petty wars. By the end of the fifteenth century the city states had become splendid centres of learning and art; the greatest masters of the artistic High Renaissance were reaching maturity—and then suddenly, in 1494, it seemed as if the history of Italy were turned back a thousand years to the time of the barbarian invasions. The French poured over the Alps from the north-west; the forces of the imperial house of Hapsburg came from the north-east and, from the south, from their province of Sicily, came the Spaniards.

All Italy was to suffer from successive waves of invaders in the years that followed 1494, and it is small wonder that a politician like Machiavelli should look to the foundations of his Florentine constitution to analyse the reasons for its sudden insecurity. The ruling house of Sforza in Milan began the sequence of events which was to change the Italian political scene. In an attempt to gain advantage over rival Naples, Lodovico Sforza invited Charles VIII of France to cross the Alps and back with force Charles's claims to the throne of Naples. This event—a moment of crucial importance for the history of Italy—coincided with a period of crisis in Florence. There the long rule of Lorenzo dei Medici had closed with his death in 1492, ending the period of Florence's greatest stability and security. Lorenzo had been responsible in many ways for the peace of Italy during his ascendancy, playing the game of Italian politics with unrivalled skill. Importantly, too, his régime combined two principles in government that were to continue to occupy the minds of Florentine political thinkers: despotic rule and republican fiction. In fact, Florence had remained relatively stable under the personal control of Lorenzo the Magnificent, while democratic suscepti- bilities had been appeased by outward appearances of republican- ism. These two principles, despotic power and shared power, provide the central political tension in Florentine political think- ing throughout the years that followed; they constitute a central opposition in the science of political thought that Machiavelli was to found, stemming from his closest acquaintance with political life in those years, and have not lost their relevance today.

Another coincidence occurred in Florence at this time which provides another aspect of the background to constitutional crisis. Girolamo Savonarola, the moral conscience of Machiavelli's age, prophesied from the pulpit the impending doom of the Florentine state as a direct result of the wickedness of its citizens. He foretold evils both spiritual and political that would befall the city unless the Florentines mended their ways, and spoke of an avenger sent by God to punish wrongdoers. In answer to this prophecy, as it were, Italy was invaded by Charles VIII in 1494. In a fury of moral enthusiasm Lorenzo's heirs were driven from the city and a republican constitution re-introduced. The sequel is well known: Savonarola's lesson of medieval simplicity, his doctrine of hell-fire and his republican preachings were unacceptable to Alexander VI, the worst of Renaissance popes, and Savonarola was put to death for heresy after the usual extorted confession. Savonarola represents, in his unprecedented ascendancy over Florentine political life for a time, the moral conscience in the debate, a conscience which Machiavelli was to exclude from an active participatory role in his 'utilitarian' concept of politics.

But we must look more closely at Florence herself to understand the positions Machiavelli takes in his more celebrated works—in particular, at the constitution of the city, and its oscillation between despotism, oligarchy and the participation in government of the middle class, for it would be a mistake to consider Machiavelli simply as an innovator in a vacuum. The substance of his reflections on politics derives from the prejudices and fashions in political thought that characterised his generation.

After the fall of the Medici, the reaction against despotism gave rise to the Florentine *Consiglio Maggiore*, or grand council. This institution derived in broad outlines from the *Maggior*

Consiglio, or great council, of the Venetians. Lorenzo's régime had embodied various consultative organs of government. Some of these, like the *Consiglio del Comune* and the *Consiglio del Popolo*, originated far back in the history of the Florentine state; others, like the Council of Seventy and the Council of One Hundred, had been introduced by the Medici. These last had ensured the virtual control over the city's policies by Lorenzo, since they were composed mainly of aristocratic pro-Medici Florentines. Now, in 1494, a grand council proposed to share political power among a much larger proportion of the populace, and the outward and visible sign of this change was the construction of a great hall for its meetings. Constructed to compete in splendour with the home of the *Maggior Consiglio* in Venice, the hall became the centre of the famous competition between Leonardo and Michelangelo for its frescoes.

But the wheel turned again. In 1512, the Medici returned to Florence; the grand council was abolished and its hall destroyed. Florence returned once again to a form of despotic rule. In the interim the city had attempted to live under a republican constitution. Machiavelli had risen to political prominence as secretary in the chancery, a servant of the republic. So it was this period of tension and debate, of democratic institutions—sandwiched between two periods in which power in Florence resided almost wholly in the aristocratic ruling class in the city—which provides the practical experience behind *Il Principe* and the *Discorsi*. This period (1494–1512) saw a kind of uneasy truce between those two principles (to simplify: aristocratic and democratic) that we have described. Now that the middle class, in its new and economically powerful form, had been admitted to a share in the process of government, it was only natural that dispossessed aristocrats should look for a return to their former prestige. So we find a tension or dialogue in the Florence of Machiavelli's maturity between the aristocracy and the middle classes.

Internal tensions were matched by dangers from outside.

Cesare Borgia, the son of Pope Alexander VI, was a constant menace to the peace of central Italy as he rampaged up and down the peninsula, adding city after city to his conquests until the death of his father in 1503. The struggle between France and Spain on Italian soil continued; Louis XII invaded Italy at the head of a French army in 1499, and the Spaniards appeared in Naples. Florence was, as always, in the geographical centre of these antagonisms.

From Machiavelli's Florentine background, we come to the writer and his works. How should one read Machiavelli and what were the principles which he enunciated? The most important event in his life was the return to power of the Medici in 1512 and the consequent abandonment of republicanism. As Machiavelli had been associated with that government, he was at once deprived of office, imprisoned for a while, and finally confined to a farm outside the city at Sant'Andrea di Percussino. This enforced exile gave him the freedom to write the works for which he is famous: *Il Principe*; the *Discorsi sopra la prima deca di Tito Livio*; *La Mandragola*; the treatise on war, *Dell'Arte della guerra*, and the *Istorie Fiorentine*. At that moment the active politician became the writer, but Machiavelli continued to concern himself with politics throughout his life. He scorned the literary life, and it was that conviction of the supremacy of action over contemplation which brought qualities of immediacy to his works. He became a writer *faute de mieux*, never abandoning his hope to return to the centre of Florentine political life as soon as circumstances proved favourable.

The dedication of *Il Principe* (to Lorenzo) is indicative of Machiavelli's underlying convictions; his aim was to analyse the actions of great men from his personal experience of Florentine politics and from his reading of classical examples of political success. Personal experience, then, and the example of the past— Machiavelli's own observations supported by the precedents of classical Rome. To these we must add particularly the principle of force in politics. Machiavelli wrote from the standpoint of one who had lost a cause; he had seen the republican constitution—of which he had been part—replaced by Medicean ascendancy. He had noted that this replacement had been worked through the superiority of Spanish troops. The abandonment of the *condottieri* system of mercenary soldiers and the establishment of a national militia, with the interests of the state at heart and dependable loyalties, was the only road to national security, he wrote repeatedly.[3]

If we are not to have a mistaken idea of Machiavelli's politics, it is important to look at *Il Principe* and the *Discorsi* together. It then becomes clear that he is far from being the apostle of cruelty, immorality and tyranny that tradition has painted him. In barest essentials, *Il Principe* is about the conditions necessary for a prince to rule effectively. The *Discorsi*, in spite of its humanist façade of a commentary on a classical work, is about the conditions necessary for a republic to succeed as a form of government. That Machiavelli was a republican comes as a surprise to those who have read only *Il Principe*, but it is after all consistent with the kind of government with which he had been associated.[4] He wrote *Il Principe* in response to a specific need: hoping that the treatise might find favour with the Medici and win him a return to active political life. If we imagine him in a contemporary situation—a party-of-the-left politician, defeated in election, who writes a treatise for the party-of-the-right in power, hoping for a post in the administration—then Machiavelli's position becomes clear. He sets out to analyse the conditions necessary—not ideal nor approved by any moral or other standard, but expedient according to the conditions prevailing in his day—for the retention of power by a new prince, once that power has been obtained. His formula is therefore a set of rules from experience rather than the conventional mixture of experience, Christian morality and humanist ideals; and in this lies its novelty.

The problem of the new prince was topical and pressing when

Machiavelli wrote *Il Principe*. In fact the new pope, Leo X, a Medici himself, was likely to want to establish his relatives in positions of princely power, just as Alexander had done for Cesare Borgia. So this piece of advice was very much to the point at the moment when it was written. In the *Discorsi*, too, he was answering a current need—for who knew what formula of government the Medici, now returned to power, would need to retain control, bearing in mind the example of Lorenzo? In short, these two works taken together provide a panoramic view of opinion about political realities and institutions current in Machiavelli's day, from the government by the few to the government by the many. Machiavelli could not have realised how prophetic this dualism was to be for the political history of Europe.

Machiavelli expressed other themes that were part of the political climate of his time. During the Florentine republic there had been much discussion of whether a government should be broadly or narrowly based. In the *Discorsi* he takes up this problem again, asking whether a broadly based constitution resulted in the election of the right leaders and whether such an administration tended to respect treaties better or worse than an oligarchy.[5] Again, Machiavelli's theories on the use of force are the results of debates of his day. Man's natural tendency is towards self-interest. How, then, is it possible to harness this impulse to the machine of the state to the greatest effect and with the least danger? This 'rational' approach is nowhere better illustrated than in the chapter on conspiracy. Plots have little chance of success, he writes, since plotters will betray each other when in danger to save their own skins. And there is the famous example of the power of economic realities in the preservation of the loyalty of the people: a man will more easily forget the loss of a father, wrote Machiavelli, than the loss of his patrimony. Finally, the quotation of Cesare Borgia—represented as Duke Valentino—in chapter seven of *Il Principe* was the topical example *par excellence*. Every Florentine reader would have recognised the figure of the *condottiere* princeling. But Machiavelli does not condone the piracy of Cesare; he cites his opportunism. He uses this image only as an example of political success founded on action and initiative, rather than hesitation and neutrality. Indeed Florence had had a tradition of political indecision in international affairs, preferring to await developments, the *via di mezzo*, and good relations with all parties. Machiavelli pointed to the political success of Cesare Borgia in order to demonstrate the weakness of this policy.

If many of Machiavelli's themes were his answer to problems of current political interest, it is appropriate to ask the question: in what lies his originality and universality? It is sufficient to compare the work with any contemporary political treatise to feel the weight of his literary gifts. *Il Principe* and the *Discorsi* taken together have a lucidity and incisiveness that have an almost frightening impact and modernity. In spite of his debts to contemporary political thought, Machiavelli gives an indefinable finality to harsh political realities. Never leaving the terms, structures and facts of his personal and historical experience, he yet stamps those realities into a mould that has had an enduring fascination and relevance. In logical terms, his arguments are often thinly supported by his illustrations (in fact, he freely distorts historical example), yet it is the argument, and Machiavelli standing behind it, that convinces, not any quotation that he may adduce to add weight to his thesis. And in the end, as in any literary success, it is the modernity, the relevance to all time which strikes home.

Machiavelli is most remembered for his political writing, combining a simplicity of literary expression with an acuteness of observation to provide lessons for the future. His relevance for contemporary Florence we have briefly illustrated; his vogue in the future was *Machiavellism*, a word in many languages denoting (like Petrarchism for Petrarch) two sober lessons: first, that Machiavelli's writings constitute the first foundation of the modern literature of the Italian political conscience and, second, that the inscription on that foundation stone would often be misinterpreted.

VITTORIO ALFIERI

To find creative writers of major significance in Italy who concerned themselves with man in his political state we must come to the generation that lived through the European cataclysm of the French Revolution. For the French Revolution had an effect on the political thought of the nineteenth century similar to that exercised by the Russian Revolution on our own times. In a sense, the direct descendants of Machiavelli's treatises on statecraft were the two books of Vittorio Alfieri: *Della Tirannide* and *Del Principe e delle lettere*. Alfieri was the Italian Montesquieu. His lifetime, from 1749 to 1803, spanned the *ancien régime* and the world of new nationalisms, its habits of thought and action being securely rooted in the former, but providing a prophetic commentary on the political preoccupations of the nineteenth century in Italy. His views were born of his aristocratic background under the monarchy in his home province of Piedmont, but contain the romantic fire of reaction against all tyranny that came to be associated with the prophets of the *Risorgimento* (see p 67). Alfieri's writings, therefore—his treatises on politics as well as his *Vita*, and the twenty tragedies for which he is best remembered—constitute a foretaste of the political and patriotic fervour that was to drive men like Mazzini in the struggle for Italian unity.

Like that of Machiavelli, Alfieri's political writing was the fruit of his reading and direct experience. His established debts are to Machiavelli's *Il Principe* and *Discorsi*, and to the *De l'esprit des Lois* of Montesquieu, but his travels in Europe, from Rome to London, from Russia to France, had given him first-hand knowledge of courts and rulers, and had allowed him to analyse the effects of different kinds of government. From 1772, too, his attachment to the wife of the Young Pretender, Charles Edward

Stuart, gave him direct experience of one representative of tyrannical rule. But the pattern of sources—confrontation through
travel and assimilation through reading—ends Alfieri's similarity
with Machiavelli. The cold rationalism of Machiavelli's political
calculation is supported by the academic example of historical
events both classical and recent. Alfieri's critique of tyranny, on
the other hand, is *risorgimentale* in spirit, a sure and certain step
towards Mazzini and Garibaldi and *La giovine Italia*.

Della Tirannide is divided into two books. In the first Alfieri
outlines his concept of tyranny as a form of government in which
the prince is both author and enforcer of the laws and has absolute
power in the state. He describes the effects of this régime on the
citizens: repression and fear. In the second book Alfieri depicts
the extreme results of such a process. Spiritual liberty may only
be obtained in this situation by a species of solitude—a retreat from
the corruption and servility of the tyrant's court—so that a man
may retain his dignity and self-respect unimpaired. In the final
analysis, suicide may be the only escape from enforced collaboration in the workings of tyranny. The idea of suicide is linked with
the idea of tyrannicide. And, here again, Alfieri is both ancient
and modern, using Machiavelli's philosophy of the superiority of
action over contemplation, but looking forward, perhaps, to the
assassination of Pellegrino Rossi in 1845 and the Orsini plot to
assassinate Napoleon III, or even to modern times—from Sara-
jevo to the Italian Resistance.

The thread which runs right through the work is the idea of
liberty, for Alfieri is not concerned with the analysis of forms of
government as such, nor is his intention a criticism of the governments of the Italy of his day. He is neither for nor against mon-
archies, republics and the like; rather the concept of political
liberty is a thing of passion and dedication in the yearning for a
basic political right for all men. It is the field for the poet rather
than the politician, therefore, and is almost 'personified' in the
author's dedication of the work to liberty itself. Even in this can

be seen the quality of Alfieri's political thought. For Machiavelli, liberty would be a duty in a republican constitution; for Montesquieu, freedom of action within the laws, but for Alfieri it is a cause to be fought for with the pen and the sword. It is this theme which aligns Alfieri with the poets of politics rather than with politicians. In spite of its treatise form, derived from its predecessors, the writing has the energy of passion, the dynamism of love and hate rather than the logic of political rationalisation.

The explanation of Alfieri's real concern, perhaps, is provided by his other political work, the *Del Principe e delle lettere*, which unites the problems of poetry and politics. For the poet and tyrant must necessarily be enemies. Any writer whose work reflects the principles of human and moral dignity must be opposed by the tyrant who represents, for Alfieri, the absence of these qualities. Consequently he opposes the principle of patronage and all the subservience of court poetry. He raises up the writer to a status above politics: the narrator of glory and the mouthpiece for the soul. Finally, the writer is delineated in the third book—spirit, freedom, passion and industry are the qualities to be sought—whereupon Alfieri closes his work (if any clearer identification of his standpoint were required) with an exhortation, in the Machiavellian mould, 'to free Italy from the barbarians'.

It is clear now that Alfieri's treatises are an important step in the progress of the Italian political conscience. They have not the attraction of striking originality but bear the stamp of impassioned conviction. The isolation of the man, his relative 'statelessness', is reminiscent of the great Italians of the past, of Petrarch and Machiavelli; the elevation of the writer in society to a position of pre-eminence again recalls the past and also anticipates the future, and the fire and the passion are romantic—or protoromantic, at least—in the dedication to an individual ideal, and also to the ideal of the individual, as in Alfieri's autobiography, the *Vita scritta da esso*. In this work, a swashbuckling idealisation of the writer, we have come to the phenomenon of Italian romanticism. No longer the trumpet blast of professional pride that characterised Benvenuto Cellini's attempt at self-dissection in the sixteenth century, but a genuine document of romantic solitude—with its catharsis in women and horses—that is typical of the age.[6] The myth of the poet-patriot was the gift of Alfieri to the Italian *Risorgimento* and, even if the aristocratic intellectual would have been the last actually to involve himself in conspiracy, the ideas of rebellion, violent action and anti-clericalism were to become important constituent parts of Italian political thinking in the nineteenth and twentieth centuries.

Alfieri has been much criticised for his supposed failure to conceive society in political terms; the abstract nature of his political thought—its roots in the principle of liberty rather than the practice of politics—has caused the rejection of his philosophy as negative and destructive, rather than positive and creative. But Alfieri was no politician, was never the advocate of a political system nor of a class struggle. *Libertà* is a sentiment or creed. Consequently Alfieri's treatises are hardly manuals for action, as Machiavelli's *Il Principe* was originally conceived; rather they are symptoms of the romantic preoccupation with liberty from oppression conceived in terms, almost, of a spiritual right. As such, the principle finds its true outlet in Alfieri's tragedies, particularly in *La Congiura dei pazzi* (drawing chiefly for its source material on Machiavelli's *Istorie Fiorentine*) and *Saul*, a tyrant under the spell of religion, itself an invader and oppressor (in Alfieri's view) of the free spirit. What strikes the modern reader most, however, in the whole corpus of Alfieri's writings, is the spirit of rebellion, the romantic thirst for freedom from oppression, that yearning of the late eighteenth century that the nineteenth century was to satisfy in the violence and destruction of revolution.

UGO FOSCOLO

Ugo Foscolo, unlike Alfieri, was a man of both the pen and the sword. Besides reflecting in his writing the political realities of his day, he was also part of them. Brought up by a Greek mother and Venetian father, he moved restlessly around Italy, driven by his duties as a soldier fighting in the Italian part of the French army against the Austrians and Russians, and motivated by stormy and tempestuous love affairs—a formula which suggests Byron. With Foscolo we come to the great disappointment of the Italian political conscience in the revolutionary period. He welcomed the rise of Buonaparte as a potential liberator of Italy from the yoke of oppression, addressing to him the *Ode a Buonaparte liberatore* in 1797, but was betrayed as a son of Venice by the treaty of Campoformio which handed that ancient republic to Austria.

Alfieri had died in 1803, and his political thought had been characterised by a generalised yearning for freedom from tyranny. Foscolo lived on through this period to suffer the disappointments of the Napoleonic *débâcle* in Italy. In his epistolary novel, the *Ultime lettere di Jacopo Ortis*, Foscolo expressed all the romantic fire of love, personal solitude and political passion that the autobiographical genre was to provide: in France in Rousseau's *Nouvelle Heloïse*, in Germany with Goethe's *Werther*; and there are even echoes of Edward Young's *Night Thoughts*. The *Ortis* of Foscolo is perhaps the great Italian statement of romantic values in prose, inseparable from its twin sources: the heartrending cry of the Italian romantic, disappointed in love and disillusioned in politics, and the lament of the Italian people for their lost potential freedom. The book was written in 1798 and revised in 1802, a four-year period of momentous importance for Italian political history.

In 1793 Europe was gripped by the trauma of the French Revolution. Having executed Louis XVI and Marie Antoinette and declared themselves a republic, the French declared war on Austria and her Italian ally, Piedmont. In 1796 Napoleon Buonaparte descended on northern Italy in command of the French

army to usher in a period of change and political upheaval unrivalled since Charles VIII had done the same thing in the days of
Machiavelli almost exactly three hundred years before. Napoleon
defeated the Piedmontese in Lombardy and three Austrian armies
in quick succession. Far from the hoped-for reforms, democracy
and equality and all the propaganda of the revolution, Napoleon
brought foreign domination and occupation to the Italians, ex-
tinguishing in one blow the ancient traditions of the republic of
Venice and handing her to Austria, and keeping the rest of
northern Italy for France. Thus the wheel of Italian political
fortune had turned again. Napoleon encouraged the creation of
republics in place of principalities as a concession to the idea of
liberty, but Italians soon realised that, even if the constitutions
wore a new face, their underlying realities, taxation and oppression, remained the same. By 1799 the French controlled the whole
of Italy.

Napoleon had given the Italians a species of social equality, but
not political liberty; and we should not forget that writers on
politics in that turbulent generation were concerned with the
latter more than the former. Alfieri had looked forward to freedom
of the individual from the tyranny of oppressive rule; Foscolo
now followed his lead in a specifically romantic and personal,
rather than social, ideal. His *Ode to Buonaparte* is couched in these
terms.

The *Ultime lettere di Jacopo Ortis* sums up in one work the
spirit of the age: the fusion of dreams for an Italy freed from
domination by foreigners and the romantic yearnings of the
solitary poet. The work represents the twinning of two of those
ideals which will constitute the political idealism of the *Risorgimento*: love for woman and country, and action above contemplation in politics. Foscolo saw service as a soldier in Italian armies;
he was prepared to go into exile rather than take an oath of
allegiance to Austria, and he was involved in the political struggles
of his day in a way that Alfieri never was. Clearly autobiographical

in its general idealism, *Ortis* reflects the views of the warrior-poet, and became standard reading for aspirants to Italian unity after 1815.

By the time of the reworking of *Ortis* in 1802, however, Foscolo had become a prey to despair. The idealism of hopes for Buonaparte's intervention had been chastened by experience. The book is shot through with this malaise, and weighed down by the tedium of Ortis's (again autobiographical) disappointment in love; but, in spite of this, the ideal was prophetic. Suicide for Jacopo Ortis was not a final gesture of despair as it had been in Alfieri's *Della Tirannide*. It is not the escape from all systems and the disdain for involvement that separates Alfieri finally from practical politics, but it is the new sacrifice to a cause. It represents the final refusal to compromise with a political reality which is nationally degrading, the sacrifice in battle, so to speak, that was to become part of the currency of Italian political thought in 1820, 1848 and 1860. The recent view of *Ortis* as political in its inspiration, therefore, still holds validity; the love for woman remains part of the human fabric of the work—just as Beatrice was for Dante—but secondary, in a work that expresses in full measure the exact configuration of the Italian political conscience at a key moment in the history of the Italians.[7]

Less political than the *Ortis*, though highly significant in the story of Ugo Foscolo, as well as for the temper of the times in its nostalgia for past greatness, is his greatest poem, the *Dei Sepolcri*. Its theme derives, on the surface, from a Napoleonic edict of 1804 in which the dead were to be buried unmarked by tombstones and outside urban areas. This edict—dictated by a combination of egalitarian and hygienic motives—has little importance for the depth and significance of the poem. From the initial feelings of sorrow at the passing of great men to an unmarked grave, unremembered by the ingratitude of subsequent generations, Foscolo moves out into a more general consideration of the Italian cult of the dead. Commemoration of greatness on a tombstone may serve to inspire the living; the great societies of the past have not failed to commemorate their dead, but finally time sweeps away even graveyards. It changes men and destroys civilisations. The only hope for man lies in the consolation of poetry itself, a true repose and tranquillity, and in the *Dei Sepolcri*, a major work, Foscolo has moved on from the romantic despair and pessimism of the *Ortis* to the consolation and certainty of faith in poetry.

With the despair of the *Ultime lettere di Jacopo Ortis*, and the longing for the values of ages now past of the *Sepolcri*, the pessimism of the former and the catharsis in the beauty of poetry itself of the latter, we have come to the dualism central to the work of Giacomo Leopardi, perhaps the greatest Italian poet of modern times.

GIACOMO LEOPARDI

Leopardi is best known for his *Canti*, a collection of poems ranging from the intensely personal and justly renowned *Infinito* to the longer and more polemical *Ginestra*. They provide a consummation, in a sense, of the ideas of that generation of writers which launched the Italians on their idealist path towards the *Risorgimento*. The themes of his poetry are those we have found already in Alfieri and Foscolo: romantic solitude, the sorrow of love denied and the greatness of Rome betrayed in modern times; and for Italians, particularly, the two faces of nature, the *bruto poter*, that cruel power which works towards man's destruction, and its sublime beauty which continuously demands his allegiance and worship. For Leopardi is universal in his pessimism. No longer is a petulant Alfieri content to inveigh against injustice; no longer is a Foscolo driven to despair by the successive disappointments of the Napoleonic era; Leopardi's solitude, his love and his despair speak directly across the years to become an enduring statement quite apart from his historical position astride the old world and the new. It has been said many times since the days of the critic De Sanctis that Leopardi's positive vision emerges from his negative conclusions. Rarely is his despair divorced from his manifest love for man and nature; rather each gains poetic validity from the other. Like that of Petrarch, Leopardi's poetry is about himself, but becomes instantly and impressively a valid meditation on the whole human condition.

To limit example to his poem *La Ginestra* we can see the extent to which Leopardi does and does not fit into our pattern. In the dignity and resignation of the broom to the surging power of the volcano, Leopardi elevates the 'true philosopher' to a status above life, so to speak, away from politics and the mundane reality of everyday life to a position outside it. Man should bow his head in acceptance of his destiny without futile resistance. But in the communion of mankind against nature—the formula of Leopardi's conclusion in the poem—we have a common theme with the other begetters of *Risorgimento* idealism; and, in its theme of the resistance of the individual to the forces which surround him, the final cosmic statement of Alfieri's individualism and Foscolo's rejection of compromise. The suicide suggested by Alfieri and practised by Jacopo Ortis has become fused into a poetic image; the dignity in submission of the yellow broom on the slopes of Vesuvius giving way to the inevitable, sacrificing itself to Nature's overwhelming force.

Giacomo Leopardi, in the great poems of his later years, is not a poet of the political conscience in the narrow sense; his pre-occupations are those of man in all times, and he rises above the particularised political attitudes with which we are here concerned. But he represents an important consummation of political attitudes: their universalisation, in a word.

Leopardi did indeed write the patriotic and political *All'Italia*, but it is material which hardly lifts the lament for Italy's lost glory, and the poet's hopes for her resurgence, to a universal plane. This was the young Leopardi, not yet grown to full knowledge of his age, and writing from the standpoint of the student of the past without the necessary immersion in the present. Rather it is in the other *Canti*, the private Leopardi rather than the public poet, that the spirit of the nascent *Risorgimento* emerges. Vittorio Alfieri ushered in the nineteenth century with a cry for liberty. Ugo Foscolo developed the theme with the full romantic apparatus of the epistolary novel. Leopardi lifts the themes of struggle and resignation, rebellion and death on to a higher plane in some of the most successful poetry in the Italian language. It fell to the next generation, however, to translate the political conscience of the era of Napoleon and Nelson into the politics of Cavour, Mazzini and Garibaldi.

It sometimes seems ironic that Italy's great political traumas are not accompanied by the literature of the political conscience. We have seen some examples of Italian writing that seems to prophesy the great events of the mid-nineteenth century, which we might call the literature of aspiration. When we come to Carducci, we have reached the generation which looked back, for the most part, on the events of the *Risorgimento*, perhaps the literature of reflection.

ALESSANDRO MANZONI

It would not be true to say that Italian unity did not produce its own literature, but, in the years between the first stirrings of revolt against foreign occupation in 1820 and their final consummation in 1860 and after, Italian patriotic literature did not achieve the heights and significance of what had gone before and what was to come after. The historical novel *I Promessi sposi* by Alessandro Manzoni is the exception to this, being perhaps the greatest Italian literary achievement of the *Risorgimento* years; but with Manzoni, and perhaps also with Silvio Pellico, we have a fusion of themes—the political or patriotic conscience mingles with the Catholic conscience.

Manzoni's early poem *Il Trionfo della libertà*, like Leopardi's *All'Italia*, was a youthful effusion embodying perhaps more the idealism of youth than the spirit of the time. But the later poems

Marzo 1821 and the *Cinque maggio* (written on the death of Napoleon), both coming after the key date of Manzoni's conversion to
Catholicism in 1810, are a preview of the contemporary political
conscience of *I Promessi sposi*. Liberty and independence are gifts
from God to the people, and are an expression of divine justice.
Even the *Cinque maggio* reflects this theme and the identification
of liberty with divine justice. Manzoni implies that even men
born to positions of greatness and power, like Napoleon, are
subject to man's inevitable destiny in oblivion and death, and it is
in God's plan for humanity rather than in human devices that
resides the justification for human struggles. Manzoni's place in
the Italian literature of the Catholic conscience is discussed in
Chapter 4, but the historical novel, *I Promessi sposi*, is also important for the Italian political conscience, for the historical novel
could be political by analogy. Just as the first audiences of Verdi's
Aida would apply its warlike spirit and freedom from domination
to their own contemporary political situation, so the readers of
Manzoni's novel could make the bridge between the oppression
of individuals like Renzo and Lucia and the oppression of
Italians in their own time. The spirit of the novel, its long and
sustained cry against injustice, in spite of Manzoni's meticulous
reconstruction of the seventeenth-century setting is again *risorgimentale*—a document in a minor key, because subservient to
religious and moral issues of the Italian political sensibility, just
as Leopardi's more classical poems, like the *Ultimo canto di Saffo*
and *Bruto minore*, are a transposition into a classical frame of nineteenth-century values.

Leopardi and Manzoni are perhaps farther from the political
tract than any of their contemporaries and achieve the highest
recognition as creative artists. Much more obvious mouthpieces
for the political conscience of the times were Giovanni Berchet
(1783–1851), Massimo D'Azeglio (1789–1866) and Tommaso
Grossi (1791–1853); perhaps because they mirror this conscience
at the expense of more enduring preoccupations, their work has

remained tied to its century. They are almost overtly didactic in the correspondence of their historical subjects to the politics of Italy, and the subject of their novels seems chosen to convey the message, particularly with D'Azeglio's novel *Marco Visconti*, published in 1834, which may serve as an example of the genre. Based on events in the fourteenth century, the work has lessons for the nineteenth century. Similarly his *Ettore Fieramosca* has echoes of Scott and Manzoni, but is more a document of nineteenth-century romantic patriotism than a novel. Significantly the values of individual heroism, force and nationalism achieved great popularity in Blasetti's film of the book in Fascist Italy in 1938.

SILVIO PELLICO

More worthy of mention in the circle of historical writers of political analogy is the Manzonian Silvio Pellico. For him art and life were inextricably bound together, for it was his imprisonment by the Austrians for political offences, first at Venice in the *piombi* that Casanova had made famous, and afterwards in the castle at Spielberg, that caused the production of *Le Mie prigioni* in 1832. The attractions of this work, with its obvious political critique of the Austrian occupation of Lombardy, go beyond the fascination for the stamina and survival of the individual subjected to every conceivable kind of physical hardship to the sublimation of suffering in religious faith. Pellico's crime had been his association with the *Conciliatore*, a periodical (1818–19) founded to promote liberal ideas, which immediately excited a reaction from the Austrian rulers of Lombardy. But his account of his experiences, supported by the eyewitness corroboration of his fellow-sufferer, Maroncelli, is polemical in a subtler way than D'Azeglio's work was to show. He rises above the simple denunciation of oppression and hardship to express a dignity in suffering and a universal self-knowledge through faith which brings him close to Manzoni in theme, if not in achievement.

So Manzoni and Pellico constitute a second kind of literature of political aspiration—writers whose political conscience was also an article of religious faith. They share with the minor writers Berchet, Grossi and D'Azeglio the growing tendency towards the use of history as analogy. But it is only Manzoni who finally survives the limiting historical strictures of propaganda, and *I Promessi sposi* stands alone as a novel of enduring literary significance.

THE RISORGIMENTO

The events of 1848 and the 1860s in Italy were a fulfilment of this literature of political aspiration, from its early beginnings in the romantic idealism of the Napoleonic era to the more recent specifically anti-Austrian writings. The election of the 'liberal' Pope Pius IX in 1846, the granting of constitutions by absolutist régimes, and riots against authority in a number of cities, all encouraged the state of Piedmont to take military initiative in 1848 when King Charles Albert declared war against Austria. Italy was not yet fully united in spirit, however, and disunity caused by ancient inter-state jealousies contributed to the Austrian defeat of the Italians at Custoza. But the nationalist appetite had been whetted, and the outcry for justice and freedom from oppression—a constant reality for half a century—had been, for a time at least, translated into concerted action, and liberal constitutions had been briefly tasted.

The chance came again. The Piedmontese statesman, Camillo Cavour, used the diplomatic situation after the Crimean War to gain international sympathy for the Italian cause; he pursued the principle of foreign alliances at his meeting with Napoleon III at Plombières in 1858, when he exchanged Nice and Savoy for French help against Austria. In 1859–60 Piedmont had a second opportunity on the battlefield and defeated Austria with French assistance at Magenta. Napoleon III then abandoned the cause of Italy by signing an independent treaty with Franz Josef of Austria.

Sicily was won by Garibaldi and his Thousand Red Shirts. Venice was to remain Austrian until the intervention of Prussia and Bismarck in 1866. After the defeat of the Austrians at Sadowa, Venice was finally ceded to Italy.

The momentous events of those years, both diplomatic and military, are of perennial fascination for historians. The Italian peninsula had for the first time in 1,500 years become one nation in a period of change, a 'trauma', of incomparable dimensions. The effects of these events on literature were inevitably all-pervading. Their obvious inheritors were perhaps the poets with, at their centre, Giosuè Carducci; for their recorded moments, feelings and reactions in nineteenth-century Italy are best suited, in a way, to register the immediacy of the political conscience. The novel must stand back in time, so to speak, to record broader issues on its wider canvas (see Chapter 3).

GIOSUÈ CARDUCCI

Carducci's life had the unification of Italy at its centre, as can be seen from his dates, 1835–1907. He was not without companion poets—such as Mameli, Mercantini, Prati and Aleardi—to chronicle the *Risorgimento* political conscience, but Carducci came to be looked on as the official poet of the new Italy, and his poems survive the test of time better than many by his contemporaries. Thus Carducci became the true heir of Alfieri, Foscolo and Leopardi.

His father had been politically active in the revolution of 1848 and Carducci lived through the thick of the political ferment from which the new nation emerged. He grew old in the idealism of university teaching and translated the image of the poet-patriot into the more modern poet-professor. His work is characterised by an uncompromising and fiery liberalism in its rejection of the insipidities of romanticism in literature, and of the Catholic Church in politics. He reacted against the more recent writers of his own century in favour of a return to classical models; he celebrated several moments in the political progress towards Italian unity in his poetry, became an impassioned republican and supporter of Mazzini, and attacked vehemently what he thought was the obstruction by the Vatican of Italy's logical destiny. Carducci was never content to remain on the political sidelines. He identified himself closely with a variety of dissident groups, being lucky, in 1869, to escape the severe consequences of conspiracy. He occupied various university chairs, the most important being the Chair of Eloquence at the University of Bologna. After a long and eventful life, in which amorous as well as political escapades drew strong reactions from his critics, Carducci was awarded the Nobel Prize for Literature in 1906, the year before his death.

Like many of his contemporaries, Carducci was convinced of the appropriateness of history in poetry, a principle we have seen in the novels of the Italian political conscience in his generation. The examples are legion, but *Piemonte* will serve as an example. This poem, which was an ode to the state which started the movement towards Italian unity, is typical of Carducci's fusion of historical, patriotic and sentimental values. The countryside of the region, with all the abrupt contrasts of its mountainous terrain, is bathed in the light of antique glory; the king, Charles Albert, is seen as the hero of that first military intervention and the poet Alfieri, a native of the region, symbolises the coming together of the themes of Piedmont and One Italy in his prophecy. The whole is written in impassioned, emotionally charged and high-sounding terms and raises the achievement of the *Risorgimento* to epic proportions. Alfieri announced the coming of liberty in his Piedmontese Israel, and Charles Albert fulfilled this glorious prophecy. The result is a poem which exults in the patriotism of Italians in those years and transposes incident and event into epic. Many of the major events of the 'trauma' can be read into the poem, but they are built into a close-knit complex of spiritual and political values. *Piemonte* is a poem which, like its author, is full of minor imperfections, but seems to express the charged atmosphere and the political conscience of Italians of Carducci's generation. Hardly corresponding entirely with today's taste, it none the less gives a vivid impression of political enthusiasm.

If *Piemonte* was a poem of reflection on the *Risorgimento*, Carducci also wrote political and patriotic poems of occasion. *Alla Croce di Savoia* of 1859 celebrated the voluntary annexation of Tuscany to Piedmont. Several later poems like *Il Plebiscito* and *Sicilia e la rivoluzione*, as well as those addressed to Garibaldi, expressed similar transitory moments in the progress towards unity, fixing the enthusiasm and euphoria of Italians into a poetic mould, but not significantly outliving their historical popularity. The *Inno a Satana* of 1865 was perhaps the climax of Carducci's anticlericalism, but is less satanic than it sounds, representing the progressive spirit of man in his struggle with tradition and superstition rather than the antithesis of Christianity.

Carducci was constantly the rebel and the agitator, combining poetry with pamphleteering, speechmaking and protesting, according to very modern handbooks of political activity, but he was not insensitive to other poetic currents in his century; in that turbulent epoch, mood and feeling produced some fine poetry, particularly in the more personal and reflective *Rime nuove*. In the lyrically personal *Pianto antico*, the identification of the sadness of a lost son with associations of the changing seasons, and in poems like *San Martino* or the *Idillio Maremmano* one finds a more enduring Carducci; and it is possibly Carducci's train in *Alla Stazione in una mattina d'autunno*, with its echoes of that other side of the nineteenth century, the industrial revolution, that remains with the young student approaching Carducci from the distance of the twentieth century. With Carducci's train we are reminded of D'Annunzio's torpedo-boat (see p 75) in another more brutal celebration of the poetry of steel, but the Carducci of *Pianto antico* leads straight to Pascoli.

GIOVANNI PASCOLI

Giovanni Pascoli was Carducci's younger contemporary and represents a muted tone in the literature of nineteenth-century Italy. His political conscience, though sincere, became a duty and a form in later life, and we find far less of Carducci's intimate involvement in political life. Pascoli's *Poemi del Risorgimento* (with all the familiar subjects: Napoleon, Charles Albert, Garibaldi), published posthumously in 1913, are academic exercises lacking the fire of personal conviction. Indeed it was a duty incumbent on the successor to Carducci's chair at Bologna, to which Pascoli came in 1906, to celebrate Italy's recent glories in poetry. Only one incident—Pascoli's arrest and imprisonment after involvement in the public protest at the condemnation of the would-be assassin of Umberto I in 1878—testifies to his political feelings in those years, and these were of biographical rather than national importance. Pascoli's poetry is private and personal in its best moments, and reflects feelings and sentiments at home, so to speak. The loss of a relative, the sounds of the countryside, or a mood of sadness are more intimately felt and transposed into authentic poetry than the political realities of the New Italy. Melancholy and mysticism, atmosphere and mood become the co-ordinates of his poetry.

GABRIELE D'ANNUNZIO

From the essentially private Pascoli we pass to the public D'Annunzio, a poet whose self-election as the guardian of the Italian political conscience was never in doubt. Gabriele D'Annunzio represents in his poetry, novels and plays the cultural ethos of decadence. He represents the transition from Italian romanticism and the liberal *Risorgimento* to classicism, imperialism and Fascism—in short, the passage from the nineteenth century, the era of Italian nationalist identification, to the twentieth century and its disastrous affirmation of that identity in Fascism and its consequences. In a very real sense, D'Annunzio was the prophet of Fascism and the literary counterpart to Mussolini.

At this point it is appropriate to consider what had happened since unification. After 1870 Italy was faced with a dual problem: to eradicate the deep-rooted regionalism that divided Italians from each other and fragmented and dispersed the new nation's national efforts, and to bring Italy firmly into modern times from the antique social and economic conditions which still characterised daily life. For, in a sense, unification had imposed a political unity on a collection of regions divided by centuries of tradition. Unlike the Austrians, who had found common cause and a unifying principle in the Hapsburg dynasty, Italy had never had a centre of political focus. And the industrial revolution in Europe had left Italy far behind in its expansion of industry and mechanisation, both because it had been in the interests of such states as the Bourbon Kingdom of the Two Sicilies to hinder economic progress and because Italy was still a predominantly agricultural country, lacking the natural resources and raw materials fundamental to industry.

So the Italy of D'Annunzio's generation was weak, disunited and poor, aspiring to international recognition as a European power to be reckoned with, but with a somewhat artificial unity of recent acquisition, and internal economic problems remaining to be solved. Up to 1876 the record was good. The heirs of Cavour and the party of the right had managed to avoid the worst pitfalls for an emerging nation and to lay the foundations of modern Italy. But government passed to the centre-left in 1876 in a fundamental shift of emphasis. Natural reaction against the rigours of a taxation programme designed to extricate Italy from her problems, and the deaths of King Victor Emmanuel in 1878 and of Pope Pius IX in the same year completed a process of radical change in Italian life. The generation that had united Italy was now disappearing; friction was caused on the international scene by plans to annexe Italian-speaking territory; the political emphasis shifted from right to left, its centre from the north (Turin) to the south (Rome), and the prevailing winds were blowing against monarchy and the Church and for southern rather than northern control of Italy's political destiny. So the 1870s ushered in a turbulent period in the life of the new nation. During the next fifty years the political pendulum swung to and fro. Gradually the nation struggled to establish itself on a par with other European nations for whom the mould had been set for generations. With the exception of the south, economic affairs improved, but the fashion for imperialism drew Italy inexorably into a system that was to have lasting consequences.

D'Annunzio's early life was therefore the experience of Italy's teething troubles in political turbulence and the search for national identity after unification. By 1897 he was ready for action in politics and literature, and had already forced himself on the attention of the public with a considerable volume of works and by a life-style more public than private. Scandal and controversy surrounded many aspects of his activities—the 'immoral' content of novels like *Il Piacere*, his journalistic writings, and frequent well-publicised love affairs culminating in that with the celebrated actress Eleonora Duse. Such image-building prepared Italy for his direct intervention in the destiny of his country. A stream of poems, novels and, later, plays poured from his pen in the 1880s and 1890s and epitomised one side of the great cultural struggle that was just beginning.

The late 1890s saw a turning point in the political and cultural history of Italy. The pendulum swung back from the earlier attempts at socialism to the new nationalism and, from the beginning of the new century, Italy entered a period in which her political fortunes and the career of Gabriele D'Annunzio were never far apart. Importantly one reason for this was a coming together of literature and politics, a cross-fertilisation of literary and political attitudes which had hardly been possible before.

D'Annunzio became the prophet of this movement, the literary spokesman of nationalism, force, violence and individual determinism, or the heroic possibilities of individual and personal action. Benedetto Croce, the great philosopher, historian and literary critic, became its chief critic. D'Annunzio's whole image, or myth, in life and work lead directly into Fascism, while Croce was the father of a tradition of anti-Fascist writing which we shall shortly consider.

This is why it is difficult to separate D'Annunzio's life from his work. He was first elected to the Italian parliament in 1897 on the extreme right wing, passing to the far left soon afterwards with chameleon-like rapidity. He returned from a voluntary exile in France to champion the cause of Italy's intervention in World War I, supported the Libyan war, and accomplished various spectacular feats of military daring, including the first solo flight over Vienna in 1918. After the war, he became even more closely allied with nationalistic and Fascist currents. He again 'represented' Italy's contemporary disappointment that she had not gained Fiume when he occupied it with a handful of like-minded adventurers.

As a political writer committed to the greatness of Italy, D'Annunzio cannot easily be seen as a worthy successor to Foscolo, Alfieri and Carducci. Independence and national unity had been the political themes of their commitment, and the central motif of the *patria* had been exalted as a moral and religious duty. D'Annunzio exalted not the *patria* but nationalism. He promoted the concept of the superman and the religion of force. The love of one's country had become the love of power in the competitive urges of European colonialism. The D'Annunzian hero hardly outlives the poet, therefore. He is composed of a pastiche of ancient heroes, Roman and Greek; a flavour of Garibaldian dash in an era when memories of the *Risorgimento* were overlaid with their subsequent disappointments, but mostly of D'Annunzio himself, a personality exotic and immoral, sensuous and refined, that posterity sees as more accurately reflecting the decadence of his age than the prophet in the political evolution of the Italian nation. As in the life, so in the work; D'Annunzio's writings on war have not lifted the wars of that time to literary meaning and significance. The play *La Nave* and the poetry of the *Odi navali* celebrate the importance of sea-power in drama and poetry but have a dated ring, as do speeches like *Il libro ascetico della giovane Italia*, *Per la più grande Italia*, and his *Canto augurale della nazione eletta*.

But with his *Torpediniera . . .*, the poem on a torpedo-boat, the theme of war and the glorification of violence becomes the poetry of sensations. Cold steel and swift destruction, certainly, but a technical and linguistic virtuosity that reminds one of Carducci's train. Again, it is in those brief escapes from political commitment, as in the *Pioggia nel pineto*, that this skill has a more universal and appealing scope. Taken with *Meriggio*, as the rain with the sun, the powerful possibilities of D'Annunzio's poetic forms may be seen: an immersion in the elements and an evocation of every sensation at the nerve-ends.

Sensations are the keynote of this poetry, however, and remain the D'Annunzian legacy to the future. The characters of his novels all subscribe to the religion of the senses and live lives barely separate from the life of their master and creator. Andrea Sperelli in *Il Piacere* and Stelio Effrena in *Il Fuoco* express in fully rounded terms the effects of the D'Annunzian sensuality, the trimph of appetite, the irrational drive towards individual fulfilment with no care for those trampled underfoot in the process.

The hindsight of history shows clearly that the Italian political conscience in D'Annunzio has produced little literature of more than historical validity, just as the power of Mussolini ended with the fall of Fascism. In fact, the Fascist era produced a sense of alienation in many writers who withdrew from public debate about the political scene (often for their own safety), or wrote on manifestly non-political themes. The inter-war years, however, saw the rise of anti-Fascist literature, at first hesitant and for clandestine circulation, then swelling in volume and value to represent one of the most significant directions taken by the literature of post-war Italy.

CARLO LEVI

Two books that have acquired literary recognition reflect the Italian anti-Fascist conscience between the wars: Carlo Levi's *Cristo si è fermato a Eboli* and Ignazio Silone's *Fontamara*, although both were published in Italy later than the 1930s which they purport to represent. In that they pre-date the generation of writers active during and after World War II, they foreshadow the third great trauma of the Italian political conscience—the Resistance. As in other periods when national crisis and deep-seated political opposition have been generative influences on literature, the growing antagonism to Fascism produced the tensions and passions necessary for significant literature. As before, Italian writers became committed to a political point of view (the overthrow of Fascism) and, as before, their works stand apart from or above this to become comments on the human condition unhampered by their particular historical circumstances.

Carlo Levi made no secret of his left-wing commitment in *Cristo si è fermato a Eboli*. The work describes his own experiences as an internee in southern Italy where, as a prisoner of the Fascist state, he lived among the poor and economically depressed people of Matera. Even the architecture symbolises the grandiose schemes and empty rhetoric of Fascism. Don Luigino, the village schoolmaster, stands for the arrogance and mediocrity of the *petit bourgeois* raised to bureaucratic power. Mindless officialdom inflicts every kind of indignity on internee and the local populace; and, with ironic force, the author symbolises the Fascist régime's beneficent effects on the people in the erection of a communal urinal! To this symbol—a tangible witness both to the principle of waste and to the gulf which separates government and governed—Levi adds many incidents in a minor key: the state's refusal to allow him, in spite of being qualified, to practise as a doctor, the censorship of mail and the stultifying memorising of Fascist litanies which passed for education.

But the book is far more than an eloquent condemnation of the régime, for Levi leaves his political polemic when his characters confront him with aspects of Italian society that seem ageless. That society had been abandoned by successive governments—concerned only to gather taxes and enrol conscripts—in a rift that is centuries old in the south. Accelerated and accentuated by Facism, it is nevertheless a timeless set of attitudes deeply etched into the corporate personality of the southern peasant. And it is this corporate personality, primitiveness, folklore and all, that gained control from the political passion of the author. Had Levi described merely the impact of Facism, the fashionable success of his book—and nowhere more than in the English-speaking world—might not have outlived the 1940s.

Levi describes the population of his village with a deeper compassion; he is fascinated by a more enduring reality. The peasants are seen in a linear chain of symbolism from the Romans on: their civilisation is half myth, half reality. Religion, medical science and the evil eye are but one indistinct area of remote supernatural experience, and the black madonna fuses Christianity and paganism in a blurring of conventional time scales. Perhaps this ancient society with its classic heroes fits oddly into the struggle of the workers against the repression of the Fascist state, but possibly the story has carried its author beyond polemic. Further, it may be that the charge of self-idealisation in the missionary zeal of the Christ/Levi protagonist in the wasteland of southern Italy is not wholly unjust. However this may be, it is the furniture of the work which dignifies the protagonist, not the salvation—or, at least, medicine and pictures—that he brings to the people of Matera.

IGNAZIO SILONE

In contrast with Levi's northern origins, Ignazio Silone is a product of the society which his books inevitably portray. Like Levi, his commitment to politics is unequivocal and unquestioned, and it was opposition to Fascism that provided the spur to literary creation. *Fontamara*, his best-known novel, describes the struggles of the people of a village in the author's native Abruzzi against the bureaucracy and inhumanity of the Fascist state. However, his treatment differs significantly from that of Verga (see p 108) and Levi. Verga's compassion for the Sicilian peasant was in one way the novelist's reflection on the tragedy of the *Risorgimento* in Sicily; Italian unity had left the southern agricultural labourer little better off in political inertia and economic depression. Levi's portrait of southern peasant society is in essence a portrait, a richly coloured picture of a primitive society by a gifted observer. That society was now oppressed by Fascism, but it had always been oppressed by someone. Silone's sympathy for his oppressed *cafoni* is not the picture of primitive attitudes but the delineation of a political class, a deliberate attempt to give an artistic physiognomy to a group dispossessed now in a specifically political sense. *Fontamara* is therefore not a novel of the *Risorgimento*, nor simply an anti-Fascist protest, but an artistic result of the Russian Revolution, an inquiry into the fundamental premises of the moral and political conscience in the twentieth century.

Fontamara describes the struggles of the peasants against the misappropriation by authority of the waters of a stream vital to the lives and crops of the workers. In a series of carefully modulated encounters, the author reveals the characteristics of the Fascist régime not with the academic detachment of Levi but with impassioned identification, a kind of suppressed fury born of commitment. The simplicity and naturalness of the peasants are the mouthpiece of the book. They exude the heroic resignation of the Marxist proletariat, here living in believable flesh-and-blood terms, when faced with the Fascist bureaucracy. The novel is utterly convincing in its picture of the weaknesses and strengths of humanity, the opposition of town and country, and the fullness of humour and tragedy. Politics as such do not intrude but provide the implicit co-ordinates of all action—that is to say, one can explain the action, the renunciation of the leader, the various encounters between *cafoni* and the law, bureaucracy and so on, all by reference to a political framework. The novel remains a moving account of resignation and struggle, registering in artistic terms the distance between Marxism and Fascism.

Of course, there are flaws. Does not simplicity occasionally border on stupidity—for instance, where the *cafoni* are duped by their lawyer? Is not the whole a little skeletal, lacking Levi's fullness of characterisation? Certainly there is the throb of life in the book, the convincing warmth of real people in the dignity of resignation and silent protest at injustice. Solutions are not given, but the specifically political problems of liberty and authority, dogma and truth, organisation and participation are investigated and filled with a valid artistic and human content. In this, the work rises above the specifically political to capture something permanent and enduring in Italian life. In its protest against injustice and incomprehension the novel mirrors, as do Verga and Levi, that centuries-old separation of the southern agricultural labourer from most western European cultural currents. Perhaps in this permanence lies the artistic integrity and coherence of *Fontamara*.

Since *Fontamara*, Silone has moved out in broader directions, encompassing a more moral and Christian ethic within the framework of his overall political preoccupation. Not by chance, in *Vino e pane*, Pietro Spina, the returned émigré opponent of the Fascist régime, conceals his political opposition in the habit of a priest to become Don Paolo Spada. But Pietro's gradual disillusionment with the dogmatic conformism of Communism reflects

Silone's own impatience with passive acceptance, and the point has been made that this becomes a moral question in *Vino e pane*. The divergence of participation and authority is a problem suffered not only by Pietro but also by Don Benedetto, the true priest, whose rejection of the principle of compromise on moral issues in an atmosphere of medieval purity of values looks forward to Silone's principal mouthpiece for a primitive, Franciscan and untarnished Christian ethic in Celestine V in his *Avventura di un povero cristiano*. Pietro Spina in hiding, disguised as a priest, offered further possibilities, for his attempts to solve the problems of the primitive community which shelters him provide a further insight into Silone's passionate concern for the repressed and downtrodden—in short, for the *cafoni*. The artistic possibilities of the combination of priest and communist—an unlikely combination in the Italy of real life—gave Silone his platform in the novel for this plea for humanity and justice. The novel's sequel, *Il seme sotto la neve*, continues Silone's dialogue between politics and Christianity. From Pietro's political commitment there grows a mysticism and a kind of primitive Christianity. In all his works, culminating in the recent play, *L'Avventura di un povero cristiano*, based on the historical figure of the medieval Pope Celestine V, we find the same urgent preoccupations, the same pressing dialogue. Silone provides an accurate register of some of the deepest problems facing Italian society, and particularly its political conscience, from the 1930s to the present day: the experience of Fascism, the alternative in Communism, the moral problem of choice between human commitment to the eradication of injustice and party commitment, and the place in twentieth-century society of the religious conscience.

Silone's play has brought us up to 1968, with its undoubted overtones of the papacy of John XXIII and Vatican II; he indeed represents a significant if lonely view of the Italian political conscience in those years. A parallel development in the literature of this theme is that reflecting the third great trauma of modern

Italy—the Resistance—and for this we must return to World War II.

THE RESISTANCE

It is difficult to exaggerate the effect of the war on Italy. It was the climax for most Italians of the failure of Fascism. Even if Mussolini's régime from 1922 had brought such incidental benefits as social security, in free medical care for poorer workers, and extensive land reclamation and resettlement, his foreign policy and the loss of political liberty in the country gradually discredited the system. Mussolini invaded Ethiopia in 1935 and conquered a large piece of Africa for the Italian empire; in 1936 Italy supported General Franco in the Spanish Civil War, helping to establish Fascism in Spain by 1939, and in June 1940 Mussolini joined Hitler against the allies, convinced that Italy's prestige and glorious future lay in an alliance with the fortunes of Nazi Germany.

Italy's contribution to the first phase of the war brought her unmitigated disaster; her armies in Greece and North Africa failed, and the one sent to Russia was virtually destroyed. By 1943, all Italians fighting in North Africa had been captured. Food shortages and factory strikes characterised life at home, and allied bombing was beginning to take its toll on Italian cities. By July 1943, Mussolini had fallen. Outvoted by the Fascist party and arrested, he then saw the party dissolved by Marshal Badoglio who proceeded towards a peace with the allies.

The high point of Italy's political trauma—8 September 1943—is a date etched deeply into the consciousness of the novelists who wrote about the Resistance. The armistice of 8 September divided Italy into two parts: the south was in the hands of the allies, with Italians recognised as co-belligerents against the Germans, while the north still suffered under Mussolini (whom the Germans had helped to escape) from his headquarters on Lake Garda. The classic symptoms of Italy's centuries-old malaise were thus reborn: division, occupation and civil strife, with the country the theatre of conflict between two outside powers in a world-wide struggle.

The Resistance from 1943 to 1945 involved not only those dedicated opponents of Fascism who had been gnashing their teeth in impotent fury since the 1920s, but also many Italians whose natural susceptibilities were outraged by the situation into which Fascism had brought the country. Further, the brigades formed in most Italian cities after the 'partition' of 8 September collected men and women of all ages and classes, and most political colours from Communists to Christian Democrats. Indeed the heterogeneous nature of the movement, with the underlying possibility of Communist control after the war, was a rich field of conflicts for the Resistance novelist.

Like the writers who lived through the other traumas of Italy's political history, the generation which suffered under Fascism from 1920 to 1945 had undergone a very special experience. Their young lives had been rich with drama, conflict and tragedy. They had seen the nation humiliated and they had fought their own individual—and perhaps more intimate and terrifying—war with the partisans against the retreating German forces and Italian Fascists. Many writers felt the need to fix in the novel form their experience of war and resistance, to record their experiences and the emotions generated in the extended narrative form. The meeting between lived experience and narrative expression has come to be called neo-realism in Italy and, while it does not explain all the variety of Italian postwar writing, it may serve as an introduction to one significant current.

Thus the furniture of the Resistance novel is guerilla warfare, sabotage, *rastrellamenti* (mopping-up operations), individual heroism, executions and the romantic attachment to a bandit existence in the hills. For Italians the Resistance novel has provided an antidote to national shame and a characteristically individualist concept of struggle in adversity. The theme of the heightened political conscience, therefore, given the potency of this trauma, surveys a significant range of postwar Italian writing.

Neo-realism, or the return to a more intimate involvement in art with the realities of everyday life, invites discussion of Elio Vittorini and Cesare Pavese.

ELIO VITTORINI

Vittorini's *Uomini e no*, an early example of the Resistance novel, had all the individualism of the author's technique. It describes the adventures of a group of Milanese partisans in the winter of 1943, contrasting the mildness of that winter with the bloody realities of occupation and armed guerilla resistance. The character N2 and his band emerge as cyphers, symbols of commitment to active protest, reflecting both the necessity of concealment of identity and the view that men are men or non-men in their capacity for sacrifice and commitment. The technique follows Hemingway—a combination of stark action and the repetition of meaningful slogans reflecting Vittorini's close acquaintance with American literature—but the novel is pared down to an almost too skeletal framework of political commitment, lacking the flesh and blood of character delineation to make it human. Even love is a political gesture. The 'musical' repetition of themes adds convincing strength to the book's message but reinforces the grey atmosphere in which political dedication seems the only human activity of relevance.

Conversazione in Sicilia uses similar techniques but is a novel in a different class. Describing the return journey of a young Sicilian, Silvestro, to his places of origin, the work succeeds in bringing new vigour to the novel of political commitment. The characters symbolise a full range of political attitudes, from the Fascist police spies he meets on the train (*Coi baffi* and *Senza baffi*) to the *Gran Lombardo*, Silvestro's Virgilian guide on his Dantesque journey through his past. The possibility of a political catharsis in writing is perhaps symbolised in the episode with Ezechiel, who keeps notes; as the meeting with the knife-grinder perhaps stands for the teeth of the revolution—'perhaps' because Vittorini's allegory and symbolism are consistently diffuse throughout the novel, allowing a broad range of interpretation. The protagonist's mother is a prime example, representing charity in a quasi-religious pattern of allegory; she dispenses injections to the needy in the village, brings her son to a fuller awareness of his present and future self, and is described in a re-evocation of childhood memories (melons, the smell of herrings, a continuing relationship with dead relatives) that give her an almost universal brooding presence in the novel. The concealment of its political message behind a web of literary allusion and allegory gives it a unique force and brings the novel close to poetry or music. The rejection of Fascism, sympathy for the oppressed and the feeling of political frustration of Silvestro's 'abstract furies' are sensed, not communicated, in a synthesis of the vague and the concrete. The ill-defined symbolism of the book is in stark contrast with the concrete setting for the action. Silvestro's search for his political and moral self is centred in a world of oranges, dusty streets and primitive houses in rural Sicily. There is perhaps no novel in modern Italian literature which combines so successfully the energy of political commitment with a strikingly effective technique.

CESARE PAVESE

Cesare Pavese shared Vittorini's experience of Fascism and war, but his concerns lie in other directions. He was not content to capitalise on the superficial values of drama and adventure of the Resistance, but examined the conscience of the intellectual when faced with a war situation. In his short story *Il Compagno*, political commitment is seen as a moral state, a more complex thing than party commitment, and non-alignment is just one facet of the more universal problem of solitude. In his *Carcere*, Pavese describes his experiences as a prisoner of the Fascist state, as Levi had done, but again the war is a peg on which to hang the individual's choice between identification and participation—or renunciation and rejection. Finally, in *La Casa in collina*, the war itself becomes the focus of Pavese's examination of the individual conscience. Commitment in alliance with the partisans is juxtaposed with rejection of collaboration in a world whose values have become total anathema, and where the positive results of participation are never really clear. The central character, Corrado, is continuously buffeted by this question of conscience: should he join the partisans or reject the system? The promptings of his conscience are progressively documented by the commitment of his lover, Cate, and the gesture of his young son, Dino, who flees to join the partisans in the hills. The struggle is set in Pavese's home environment in Piedmont and its emotional force is enhanced by a deep spiritual relationship with the countryside. Pavese's preoccupation with responsibility and involvement invades all his work and, in its pessimism, questions the very values on which the Resistance movement was built. He can find no answers to questions about the useless suffering caused by the war, and his novels are an eloquent comment on the aimless, valueless society devoid of ideals and direction which followed the trauma of the war in Italy.

VASCO PRATOLINI

Both Carlo Cassola and Vasco Pratolini wrote novels based on the Resistance; again, some strong contrasts are immediately evident. Pratolini's *Cronache di poveri amanti* is in the Vittorini image in that it is driven by the energy of political commitment, but it is in fact set in the earlier period of Fascism in the 1920s. Clearly, however, the polarisation of Fascist and non-Fascist attitudes that the Resistance constituted was an important element in its gestation, for it adopts the currency of guerilla tactics in use in 1943. Pratolini's novel stands at the opposite end of the scale to that of

Pavese. Pavese's works are portraits of the intellectual, revolving round the delineation of a central character, whereas the *Cronache di poveri amanti* describes a whole society, fitting together the many mosaic pieces of the working-class Via del Corno in Florence. In the delineation of this microcosm of Italian society, a narrow street inhabited by over fifty characters, Pratolini painted a huge canvas of everyday life in an Italian city under Fascism. Gradually the Fascist characters, symbolised by the obscure, rootless Carlino, and the anti-Fascist characters, led by Maciste, the blacksmith, emerge in their contrasted colours from this complex urban jungle. Pratolini is not concerned with the writer, the intellectual in a strife-ridden society, but with the simple attitudes of the working class. Not for him the doubts about the dogmatism of Communism, but rather the values of social cohesion in the politically impotent inhabitants of the Via del Corno. The 'resistance' gesture of Maciste in the attempt to extricate a leading anti-Fascist from the attention of the blackshirts, and the ensuing motor-cycle chase, is worthy of the best heroic delineation of the partisan offered by the Resistance novel.

Far from the somewhat arid idealism of *Uomini e no*, Pratolini's politics in the novel is the devotion to people, to social ideals, to common everyday lives. The political moments of his characters' lives are not the main fibre of the novel's texture, but are incidents like any other in the colourful lives of the blacksmith, the insurance salesman and the prostitute. It is this realism which lends force to the ideological struggle in the novel, setting it against a natural background of seething humanity. This background is full of the author's compassion for a political class. Pratolini describes not only the struggle against Fascism but also the permanent preoccupations of an Italian slum: woman and the family, the distrust for authority in any form, the disgust with violence and the reluctance of many Italians to associate and form parties or affinity groups.

CARLO CASSOLA

Cassola's novels of the Resistance demonstrate, as did Pavese, a more sceptical attitude towards the affirmation of anti-Fascist ideals in the Resistance, for he depicts the fate of the middle class during those traumatic years which culminate in World War II. In *Fausto e Anna*, Fausto is a bored youth and the Resistance later provides him with a cause to espouse. He affects anti-bourgeois tastes, vague literary ambitions and a sense of emptiness and rootlessness typical of his generation. His love for Anna, which provides the main thread of the novel, is linked with his gradual self-realisation, and her rejection of him in favour of a boring marriage throws him into the arms of the partisans. His membership of the brigade completes the process of self-discovery in disillusionment with theoretical Communism and distaste for the blood and guts of guerilla warfare. This again throws into relief the diversity of beliefs and origins which characterised any one partisan band.

So the framework of adventure in the novel is the setting for the examination of psychology. The sniping, the execution of a Fascist and Fausto's failure to revel in the camaraderie of the movement point the disaffection of the character with the Resistance and the disillusionment of many Italians after the war. The Americans are hailed as liberators, but they soon disarm the partisans; it seems as if one occupation is to be replaced by a different domination, and that Italy must slip back again into her traditional subject position.

If Fausto and Anna represent the middle class, do they represent anything more? An attitude has been documented which rings true, but the characters leave one dissatisfied. It is almost as if the novel were a conscious effort to deflate heroic aspects of the Resistance by juxtaposing them with the other side of the coin, to provide an antidote, as it were, to the atmosphere of epic struggle and clear shining objectives painted by many Resistance novelists. Neither Fausto nor Anna really emerges as a fully credible character in a literary sense.

ITALO CALVINO

As a work of the Resistance, the novel of Italo Calvino, *Il Sentiero dei nidi di Ragno*, stands apart from those already discussed, because of its unique viewpoint. In a way not dissimilar to Gunther Grass's more recent *Tin Drum*, the novel sees the political and social realities from the point of view of a boy—aged fourteen, not three, in this case. In its pages Pin grows to maturity through his contacts with the partisans. Their heroism and self-sacrifice are to him revelations of the facts of the adult world; they breathe an atmosphere of hopeful optimism into the novel and provoke the thought that the Resistance might herald a new society reborn after the squalid horrors of Fascism and the war. Some detachment from specifically ideological objectives is seen, but not, as Pavese had described it, with pessimistic conclusions. Calvino's struggle is the striving of all Italians to free themselves from the dilemma into which the twentieth century had thrown them. As Pin grows up, he finds friendship and trust in his partisan friends; his identification with them, symbolised by the unearthing of the treasured pistol from its hiding-place, perhaps points to the newer, younger society that may enjoy not only freedom from Fascism and German occupation but also a release from the permanent ills of Italian society: corruption, exploitation and ignorance. In this novel, too, there is a meeting point between two stylistic influences. That energy of political commitment we have been describing as an important formative influence on the Resistance novelist here comes face to face in fine balance with a genuine fable-like simplicity, a childlike delight in imagination and narration for their own sakes. This was to develop and expand in Calvino's later works to become a principal stylistic feature, but it here combines with the urgency of lived experience to make *Il Sentiero dei nidi di Ragno* a refreshing literary experience. Pin is described with humour, irony and psychological penetration. The atmosphere of fable or legendary quality of the author's style is exactly in tune with the epic quality of the adventures described, with the whole chivalric apparatus of the struggle by primitive means of an oppressed minority against a dominant majority. Perhaps because of this happy conjunction of theme and stylistic inventiveness, *Il Sentiero dei nidi di Ragno* is one of the most literary manifestations of writing on the Resistance to emerge from Italy.

It may be that a meaningful pattern emerges from this brief survey of the literature of the Italians in which the dominant theme was political. First, as we have seen, the best in political literature tended to accompany the worst in political fortunes. The energy of political commitment was always aggressive: Machiavelli wrote against his time in vindication of political exclusion; Alfieri and Foscolo wrote eloquent condemnations of tyranny and oppression; Silone was primarily motivated by his opposition to Fascism. Then the permanent malaise of the country has been its occupation by outside forces, from those of Charles VIII in the 1490s to those of Nazi Germany after 1943. In the literature of this theme, at least, peace and prosperity have never prompted political writing of passion and conviction.

From the point of view of literature, the problem remains: does a book with intent to persuade or edify qualify as art? In modern times, the line between art and propaganda has become increasingly more difficult to draw. Machiavelli's comments on the specific politics of his time are a timeless commentary on human nature and on the fundamentals of man in society; Silone mirrors the problems of his age in a series of novels which are true works of the imagination; and Vittorini achieved the perfect marriage between political energy and artistic method in *Conversazione in Sicilia*. The modern Italian writer is not afraid of commitment and alignment.

Notes to this chapter are on p 175.

CHAPTER 3

Social Change

The literature reflecting changes in Italian society goes hand in hand with moments of national crisis and excitement in the history of the Italian people. Social change—in the context of family, class and national life—is the outcome and also the portent of great political events in the nation's history. So there will always be a relationship between the literature in which the dominant theme is political and that writing—often separated in time from the major political changes themselves—which mirrors important changes in attitudes, the structure of society and manners.

Thinking back to the founders of Italian literature, it becomes clear that the literature of social change paints on a large canvas. Man in his political state is concerned with government, economics and ideology. In his social state, he is concerned with how he lives, his relations with fellow men and family, and his immediate social context, be it village or piazza, salon or court. A glance at an Italian motor car or a family home is sufficient to identify an enduring concern with style. Italians have always concerned themselves with how things are done, and their social attitudes have retained certain characteristics down the centuries. So for literature reflecting this concern, principally the novel and drama, a large canvas will be needed. Our task will be to identify aspects of social change in the works of major writers, stressing the social values of Italian society that have found permanence and stability in the fabric of the nation's daily life.[1]

BALDASSARE CASTIGLIONE

We have seen the extent to which, at the beginning of the sixteenth century, Machiavelli's political literature was the outcome of momentous changes in the nation's life, in the loss of stability caused by invasion, and the topicality of his views on government and society in the context of those important political events. It is now appropriate to look more closely at that society and particularly at Machiavelli's contemporary, Baldassare Castiglione, who expressed in *Il Cortegiano* many of the ideals of that society. In this work, we shall find the effects on the lives of Italians of humanism, culture, and theories of behaviour rather than of war, invasion and instability, for *The Courtier* is a milestone on the long journey from chivalric ideals, courtly love and the legend of the Middle Ages to the affirmation of man's individual presence and the possibilities of self-fulfilment in the Renaissance. The book reflects and signals the change from a theocentric to an anthropocentric habit of thought, and with this the social change from a society where man's rightful place was as a constituent of a medieval system to that where he became his own model and ideal.

Of course, this is simplified and generalised; in the Italian Renaissance as many examples of freedom and non-conformity can be found (Michelangelo, Cellini, Aretino) as those which reflect conformity with Castiglione's ideals (Raphael, Bembo, Ariosto), but through them all runs a current of affection for a new society founded on the individual achievements of man.

Castiglione was himself a courtier. Growing up within the framework of court patronage, humanist circles of learning, embassies to foreign courts, he crystallised the ideals of his generation in his most famous work. These were also the ideals of his time: the linguistic theories of Cardinal Pietro Bembo, the neo-platonism of Ficino and Pico della Mirandola, the government advocated by Machiavelli in the *Discorsi* and *Il Principe*, and the ideal of universal man of Leonbattista Alberti. But these theories are points of departure for Castiglione in *Il Cortegiano*. He elaborated on the theories of his generation and stamped them into an individual mould that becomes the picture of a society and the physiognomy of an ideal. Thus Castiglione was for man's view of himself what Machiavelli was for his view of politics in the Renaissance: both the codifier of principles and the idealised expression of present reality. It often happens that the modern student's first acquaintance with the Italian Renaissance is a visual one: the harmony and refinement of a Raphael portrait, or the power and pride of Michelangelo's 'David'. The *Cortegiano* represents the literary treatise on these ideals, or the pattern book of man in his social state that was to have far-reaching repercussions.

What were those ideals and in what sense do they reflect social change? It may be objected, first, that the courtier ideal represents the image of a tiny minority of Renaissance society with the good fortune and ability to play a part in the web of patronage surrounding courts like that of Urbino; and this indeed is the most obvious target and frame of Castiglione's work. But the society of which he was part had adopted the new principle of aspiration to perfection. In this, the *Cortegiano* symbolises a range of endeavour much wider than the rigid ambitions of a small group of talented *literati* with aspirations to court patronage. The limitations of the courtier in the work are characteristics of Castiglione's illustration: his principles are valid over a broad social spectrum, and were to be taken up by Giovanni della Casa in his *Galateo* and others in this broader spectrum.

The ideal courtier was to be of noble birth, expert in arms and horsemanship, strong, daring and generally skilled in military matters. The soldierly image thus provided a manly exterior for the courtier who might be called on at any time to help to defend his prince from his potentially aggressive Italian neighbours. He was to be elegantly attired and accomplished in the literary and musical arts, capable of entertaining and edifying the court in its more leisured moments. His approach to all things was to be refined, in habits of speech, dress and in his choice of associates. Humour was a desirable attribute, but should not be coarse in the presence of women. Thus far we have fairly traditional courtly attributes combining the achievements of medieval chivalry with a concept of good taste and moderation.

Castiglione proceeds with his list of desirable virtues in dialogue form, to raise the status and prestige of women from the old childbearing image to a new role of educated participation in society alongside the traditional family and moral attributes. Here he crystallises a new and emancipated ideal of woman reflected in the emergence of the poetesses of the sixteenth century, like Veronica Gambara, Vittoria Colonna and Gaspara Stampa. He reflects too the political tenacity of the women of the ruling houses of northern Italy, and the emergence of the warrior-women in the *Orlando furioso* of Ariosto and the *Gerusalemme liberata* of Tasso. Castiglione invests the ideal woman with qualities similar to that of his courtier: education and a cultivation of the arts bringing grace, refinement and social poise. It would be misleading to suggest that this portrait reflected the social position of woman in general in Italian society in the High Renaissance, but Castiglione's portrait, the symbol of its many other literary manifestations, was a statement of the ideal which was to have a vast echo in the European literature of manners.

From this Castiglione moves to the spheres of politics and love, twin preoccupations of the successful courtier. In the former, the fashion for mixed authority finds expression in the principality winning the debate with the republic, because of the supposed monarchical nature of God's relationship with the faithful. Here it is as well to bear in mind the ideal nature of the work, its moral and aesthetic standpoint as a pointer to the way an ideal courtier should see life. Machiavelli was concerned, when he discussed princes and republics, with what is and not what should be.

Castiglione sees love in the contemporary framework of neoplatonism. Contemplation of human beauty leads naturally to contemplation of divine beauty, in a passage of heightened lyrical emphasis; and, finally, the search for perfection will involve that most Italian of problems, the *Questione della lingua*, or the debate on the appropriateness of the spoken tongue in its many Italian forms to the uses of art. Here, in spite of his adoption of the neoplatonist theories of love of his contemporary Bembo, Castiglione looks back for his inspiration to Dante's *De Vulgari eloquentia* rather than to the linguistic theories of Bembo. Again the modernity of his criterion of use as the arbiter of appropriateness is striking.

Through all this runs an ideal of good taste and moderation which has done more than any other factor to cement Castiglione's reputation. This, in Italian, is *sprezzata disinvoltura*, a species of deliberately effortless grace and elegance which is to appear natural rather than studied. The courtier is to wear his learning and accomplishments lightly, and is to be the embodiment of ideals, so to speak, without seeming to try to do so.

It may be difficult sometimes to see the formulation of an ideal of behaviour as more than the fixing in one moment of a fashion for living, a transitory and evolving state, soon to be superseded by other more socially important revolutions of taste and behaviour. What of the seething and work-weary backdrop of humanity against which Castiglione's courtier struts arrogantly and assumes his pose of studied elegance? Apart from the resonance of its echoes in subsequent literature of the genre, the work is indicative of social change in as important a way as the invasion of Charles VIII heralded political change. First, the ideal of perfection of the individual—of self-training to a model in moral and aesthetic terms—divides the civilisation of Leonardo and Ariosto firmly from that society ruled by obedience to God and duty to a Lord. Of course, we cannot say that happened in 1494, nor can we suggest 1528, when the *Cortegiano* was published. But the book indicates a radical change in attitudes gradually evolving to reach this concrete formulation. Second, the ideal of the polymath was an educational ideal that was to have a long and distinguished run down to modern times. Thirdly, the concept of civic virtue, a combination of duty and moral conscience, social consciousness and personal fulfilment was again to be widely influential. Medieval man had well-defined duties towards his affinity group, the Church and the social system of which he was part. Castiglione's courtier has a duty to himself and is to cultivate a sense of style. Fourthly, the education of woman and her insertion into society as full participant, in discussion, war, poetry and so on, can hardly be challenged as a civilising and forward-looking theme, and is conceived as a practical everyday principle—far from the abstract worship of woman in the medieval courtly love ethic, or the utterly subject role assigned to her by most of western European civilisation. Of course, the ideal courtier was an aristocratic ideal; we must look to its descendants for extensions of the theme. But, in its effect on social attitudes for future generations of Italians, and seen against the background of medieval society, it represents a significant and radical change.

Apart from the picture of sixteenth-century aspirations to perfection and a style of aristocratic living provided by Castiglione's *Courtier*, there were other literary manifestations of the social changes brought about by the Italians' discovery of themselves in the Renaissance. There is not space here for a full discussion of the literary manifestations of the artists' new prestige (Cellini's autobiography or Vasari's *Lives*) or the popular currents of poetry reflecting more humble aspirations than the lofty Petrarchan themes of Bembo and his school (Aretino, Doni, Berni). But some mention may be made of the current of peasant realism represented by the comedies of Angelo Beolco, 'Il Ruzzante', because it represents the literature of social change at its other extreme from Castiglione and is part of a stream of non-classicist literature reflecting the Renaissance interest in man in his social state in all sections of society.

ANGELO BEOLCO: IL RUZZANTE

Ruzzante's plays are part of a long tradition of satire and mockery of the lower classes by the more cultivated *literati* and noble classes, but their impact goes farther than this. Ruzzante, himself an actor, was of peasant origins working also in his native Paduan dialect, and these origins provide the co-ordinates of his most significant writing. Acute observation of the country scene, peasant attitudes and the relationship between the peasant and the implacable foes of his existence—authority and destiny— give it its quality. The unchanging laws of his milieu—hunger, fear and the sexual drive—fill this framework with a throbbing vitality expressed in the uncompromising crudities of the Paduan dialect.

The brute force of these realities has always been seen in stark contrast with the more abstract preoccupations of the age: neo-platonism, Petrarchism and humanism; but its significance is also its statement of the dignity of man whatever his social milieu. The humour provided by the awkwardness of the peasant, his primitive urges, his crude expressions, when recited in the gilded lethargy of an aristocratic court, is only half the story. The other half is a genuine social comment on the tragedy of the deprived and oppressed, a picture of the customs of a society with its own antique traditions, and the relationship (or lack of rapport) of this class with the upper echelons of Italian Renaissance society. The mockery and the laughter veil social conscience—necessary stylistically for the presentation of the plays in aristocratic Venice or middle-class Padua. That conscience, remarkable for its age, links Ruzzante with other great observers of peasant realities, like Verga in the nineteenth century. If Castiglione expressed 'idealised naturalism' in the sixteenth century, Ruzzante stands for a more modern naturalism, that which documents the roots and permanent values of a peasant society slow in evolving. In that sense, his plays reflect more accurately social conscience than social change.

One of Ruzzante's *dialoghi* must serve to exemplify: the *Parlamento de Ruzante che iera vegnù de campo*—'the speech of Ruzzante returned from the war'—in which even the title conveys the immediacy and matter-of-factness of these short plays.[2] The peasant Ruzzante returns from the war, in which he had enlisted only in an attempt to escape the miseries of hunger, to find his wife allied with a more secure provider of material benefits. Disillusioned, therefore, by war, hunger and domestic infidelity, he becomes the butt of all; his fear and ingenuous outbursts against the cruelty of fate and misery document a true pathos, comic in its situation and expressiveness, but profound in its echoes and social conscience. The cruellest stroke, a beating by his wife's lover, reminds one irresistibly of Boccaccio, while the characters are described in all their breadth and depth.

THE EIGHTEENTH CENTURY

When we come to Italian society of the eighteenth century, we find a consciousness of social values that are ripe for change. With the satire of Giuseppe Parini and the 'social' comedies of Carlo Goldoni one senses a Europe setting the stage for the French Revolution. For the work of these writers reflects a consciousness of precisely those class stratifications in economic and political terms that the revolution was to overturn. Parini's attack on the idleness, futility and superficiality of eighteenth-century aristocracy goes hand in hand with Goldoni's delineation of real values, his portraits of the piazza peopled by artisans and merchants, and deflation of the pretensions of the idle rich.

The society of which Goldoni and Parini were part is visually symbolised by the painting of Canaletto and Watteau; the forms and appearances of the old aristocracies have survived without their relevance and function. The sternness and devotion to the duty of government of the Venetian patrician of the Renaissance had become the tittle-tattle of the coffee-shop, extreme fashions and masked balls in Goldoni's Venice. The Italian *salon*, like the French, collected passions and personalities devoted to the pursuit of idleness in formalised rituals. Perhaps more than anything else, it is the contrasts in this society that strike the modern inquirer, just as these contrasts scandalised Parini. Underneath the frivolous affectations of court and intellectual life there lay social strata of grinding poverty. Waste and idleness balance misery and hunger. The tourists who flocked to Italy to be entertained and to admire the faded achievements of Renaissance Rome and Florence, or to join in the carnival atmosphere of Venice, were unaware of a vast crime rate, a current of violence in both evil-doer and judiciary, and turned a blind eye to the many beggars who crowded city streets and the palaces of the rich.

GIUSEPPE PARINI

The harsh realities of this polarised society were the chief target of Parini's attack, and his weapons were satire and irony. *Il Giorno* was to have been a poem in three parts: *Il Mattino, Il Mezzogiorno* and *La Sera*; the first two were published in 1763 and 1765 respectively, while the third, lengthened and now divided into *Il Vespro* and *La Notte*, appeared in 1801, after Parini's death. The poet pretends to teach the young aristocrat, *Il Giovin signore*, how he should behave in polite society, taking the reader through a typical day in the life of the aristocracy.

In the *Morning*, the young lord wakes late, when the workers in the field have been at their labours for hours, takes breakfast, toys with lessons in the principal accomplishments of the nobility: dancing, music and French. After the lengthy ritual of his toilet and dressing, he is ready to issue into the world, protected from its ugliness and squalor by his carriage, which must not be slowed by a peasant unfortunate enough to fall under its wheels.

At *Midday*, the social context comes to life in a galaxy of lunch guests which surround the young lord and his lady and illustrate empty etiquette, futile conversation and games. Luxury and frivolity are the keynote here, and the delicacy of the food seems to vie with refinement of manners to create a thick *impasto* of eighteenth-century life. The young lord is seen as the *cavalier servente*, or *cicisbeo*, a species of formal escort for the entertainment of the lady, a period institution typical of the society and ably satirised by Parini in his poem.

In the *Evening* the young lord and his lady undertake that most Italian of all institutions, the *passeggiata*, visiting other nobles on their ceremonious progress in other gilded coaches. At *Night*, entertainment continues with a sumptuous reception at the house of a noblewoman, and the poem's canvas widens to include a broad cross-section of eighteenth-century aristocratic society.

This much on the surface: a day in the life of the young lord; but what fascinates the modern reader is the unique blend of observation and reforming spirit in the poem. Parini himself had participated in the form of aristocratic society in the Serbelloni household from 1754 to 1762, and was part of that reforming current in Milanese society known as *Illuminismo*, taking its points of departure from France. Thus his poem has the refinement and elegance of its century as well as being a biting condemnation of its excesses. The artist can scarcely resist taking pleasure in these refinements in sensuous descriptions and a sympathy of taste, while the social critic spares little in a society devoted to pleasure, entertainment and luxury from the shafts of his satire.

A further problem arises in the tone of the poem itself, for critics have often noticed its unevenness—a geography of hills and valleys—in which the poet will sometimes be carried forward by the impetus of his polemic and then languish in the rather monotonous contemplation of detail. A dualism of attitudes has been seen here. For the reader may juxtapose episodes of criticism with those of contemplation and delight, and ask: in what lies the poem's unity?

Whatever the answer, it is certain that the poem's social criticism is achieved through multiple stylistic devices. Parini visualised an ideal society motivated by the spirit of the common good and universal happiness, with a harmony both in attitude and function of the various social classes, reformed and renewed, and above all active in the pursuit of this social ideal. Every detail of the physiognomy of the *Giovin signore* contradicts this ideal; his description, life and context are stagnant, passive and unfruitful in social terms. The points where the working class surfaces in the poem are the peaks of Parini's most obvious contrast: the health, industry and honesty of workers constantly underline the lack of such qualities among the idle rich. The labourer works while the *Giovin signore* still sleeps; the servant is dismissed for failing to conceal his reaction to a bite from his mistress's lap dog; beggars crowd palace doors simply to get a whiff of the odour of cooking.

Further contrasts are implicit in many places in the poem. The labourer is inserted into a healthy countryside to symbolise man and nature in fruitful collaboration. The aristocrat is seen against a backdrop of stucco and gilt, the artifice and ornament of his meaningless and unfruitful existence. Even physical contrasts underline the point. Compare the descriptions of artisans with those tediously long accounts of the young lord and his lady. Perhaps the main impact of the poem may be seen in those extracts often anthologised as symbolic of the poem's polemic: the awakening of the *Giovin signore* and the labourer, the 'Fable of

Pleasure', which contains the roots of Parini's egalitarian beliefs, and the episode of the *Vergine cuccia*, or lap-dog. The first exemplifies the social contrast central to the poem's intention; the second, the myth or motive of equality of man fundamental to this contrast, and the third, perhaps the most celebrated example of Parini's method, the minute delineation of detail, meticulous observation and biting satire in the implicit comparison between the fortunes of the dog and the servant.

The defects of the poem we have hinted at. The marriage between polemic and poem is not always an easy one; passages of social satire alternate with periods of acute observation that have a tendency towards self-indulgence. The *Giovin signore* does not animate the poem with his life—an empty and frivolous life, maybe, but the figure in the poem is also rather empty, a package of affectations and typical attitudes rather than a living literary creation. The lack of unity is the chief defect. Nothing binds the poem into a solid artistic whole. Varied themes, variations in tone, a richness of ornamentation, all are present, but none creates a life for the poem, an internal life that is of it alone.

CARLO GOLDONI

Carlo Goldoni, Parini's older contemporary, paints a picture of his society through the comedy. As the art of social change, his plays document the rise and growth to importance of the middle class in an art form that is good-humoured rather than polemical. In literary terms, social comment is implicit rather than explicit, the irony gentle and less mannered than that of Parini, and the portrait of contemporary Venetian society more fully rounded. In 137 plays he deals with a full range of social attitudes. *La Locandiera*, *La Bottega del caffè* and *Il Ventaglio* have the advantage of typicality and established popularity in the English-speaking world.

It is important first of all to clarify Goldoni's social and political context. We have seen something of the extent to which Parini lived in contact both with the aristocratic society that he satirised and with those reforming currents known as *Illuminismo*. Goldoni's life and creativity are in a sense far from specific initiatives towards social reform; his standpoint is far more accurately described as a benevolent observation of the society in which he lived than a social criticism in the force and vigour of the term. Goldoni's plays do, however, betray a fundamental consciousness of a changing society; they contain a sincere view of the common origins of man, whatever his social status by accident of birth; they lampoon the functionless aristocracy of eighteenth-century Venice and often its poverty, and they show the author's sympathy and admiration for the values of industry and honesty among working people. But Goldoni is rarely polemical, being content, rather, to observe and relate scenes and characters from the real world about him, moulding character and situation into an artistic whole through the medium of the reformed theatre.

This real world was a changing society and the comedies reflect this change. The empty pretensions of Don Marzio in *La Bottega del caffè* or of the count in *Il Ventaglio* are not only funny in themselves. They underline a contrast between the aristocracy of Venice fallen from greatness, devoted to pleasure, of which only the formal attitudes survive, and the industry and commercial sense of the middle class, or the hard-working honesty of the artisan. Again, Goldoni satirised military valour and the art of war, and he supported the rights of women, so often the mouthpieces of his own particular middle-class morality—compare Mirandolina in *La Locandiera* with Geltruda in *Il Ventaglio*. His concern with the labourer, the servant, the fisherman shows respect for the artisan which draws him closer to Parini.

Goldoni's vision, then, was a good-natured one. Points of friction in social change—those polarities that looked forward in society itself to the cataclysm of the end of the century—are eliminated. The count, with his 'protection' and poverty, is a figure of fun rather than a candidate for the guillotine. Goldoni used the unique characteristics of the theatre to transform the values of that society in all its shades into compelling visual drama.

The necessity of observation of the real world militated against the stereotyped and 'fixed' nature of the *Commedia dell'arte*. Improvisation, character types, masks and the humour of recognition were not calculated to broaden the range of social drama. No longer were such types as appropriate to Goldoni's society as they had been, and the written comedy allowed fullness of individual characterisation as well as differentiated situations. Thus the reform for which Goldoni is most celebrated was the substitution of the *maschere*, *canovacci* and *lazzi* (masks, plot summary and character types) by comedies of character and comedies of *milieu* with a written script.

Over the vast canvas of Goldoni's production the process of this reform was a gradual one; in early comedies like *Il Bugiardo*, the title indicates a degree of abstraction, and there is but one developed character. Broadening his social spectrum—for *Il Bugiardo*, besides being a liar, was also a nobleman—Goldoni develops minor characters in the middle and artisan classes in a second stage. Finally, in the later plays the scene or scenario also assumes importance; the street and the square come fully into dramatic prominence; the coffee-shop, the workshop and the inn assume realistic proportions and seethe with the life of real people. The hammering of the shoemaker in *Il Ventaglio* is as important a part of the play's fabric as the pretensions of the count or the 'situation comedy' caused by the interminable travels of the fan. In these later or 'choral' comedies, individual characters merge back into *ambiente*; the social reality of Goldoni's latest plays takes precedence over characterisation in a mosaic presentation in which no single colour is to shine so brightly as to eclipse the general effect.

The three plays quoted demonstrate some, though not all, of

these developments, as well as inherent contrasts in Goldoni's progression. *La Locandiera*, of 1752, is often considered his masterpiece. As an early play, it develops its impact through a single characterisation, virtually, but with consummate skill and psychological penetration. The play also satirises the aristocracy, elevates middle-class skills, and speaks out strongly for the commercial ability and social expertise of woman. Mirandolina, the innkeeper, not satisfied with the court paid to her by the marquis and the count, two typical Goldonian aristocrats, sets out to win the affections of the *Cavaliere*, the only one not to have fallen under her spell. Her campaign is a *tour de force* of feminine wiles—from flattery and kindness to cooking and fainting—and its success is immediate. However, Mirandolina marries her servant Fabrizio in deference to her father's wishes and to the solid middle-class virtue of helping to keep the family business on an even keel.

La Bottega del caffè moves on from the single-character emphasis to chorality, though it retains Don Marzio, the weak aristocrat, as its central pillar. Here the *ambiente* is the play's central message— the coffee-shop being the central focus socially of a whole society. In the movements of the characters between coffee-shop, barber's shop, gaming room and inn, the picture of a street or Venetian *piazzetta* is complete. Don Marzio, the evil tongue, is here not only the fallen nobleman recognisable as a social anachronism but also the gossip, a constituent of all societies. *Il Ventaglio* has by now lost its character-pillar—a fan in its passage from character to character has become central; by 1765, society has fully re-placed characterisation in Goldoni's drama to become in this play a microcosm of Venice.

Ostensibly the play is a love story, but the plot follows the passage of the fan and is a monument to triviality. The play mirrors life itself in all its constituents, having the naturalness of speech and situation of Goldoni's society and a balanced variety of social classes. The aristocracy, in the count and baron, is shorn of function, laughably pretentious and wearing the faded costume of outworn privilege; the middle class, in Evaristo and Geltruda —melodramatic lover and wise and boringly bourgeois aunt to Candida—combines the virtues of morality and money; and the artisans, Coronato and Crespino, innkeeper and cobbler, reflect industry and honesty. The whole package of characters is seen in a half-light against the strong colours of inn, cobbler's shop and house. The episodes are played out against a rushing of figures, the noises of industry, wine barrels, the fan, the tobacco box and so on. Class meets class; they clash light-heartedly, men are vanquished by women (Evaristo controlled by Candida, Crespino and Coronato by Giannina)—in fact, everything is in its proper place in a harmony of colours and attitudes that reflect Goldoni's society. Here we are perhaps nearer to painting than to social criticism; choral comedy has less bite than the comedy of character.

THE RISORGIMENTO IN SICILY

When we come to the social change which was to follow the *Risorgimento*, it is Sicily which produces the most significant writing about society. We also move to the historical novel and the fascination of the nineteenth century with naturalism and the human comedy. For Sicily, because of the special characteristics of its previous history, was less well prepared for the radical changes brought by the unification of Italy than any other part of the peninsula. The social effects of unification were therefore more extreme—contrasted more sharply and more dramatically with the existing social order—and provided a rich field of drama for the novelist, from Giovanni Verga to Giuseppe Tomasi di Lampedusa.

A brief background sketch will serve to set the scene. The period from 1820 to 1860 of popular revolts, the agitation of secret societies and political upheaval—the *Risorgimento*—brought many changes in the social structure of Italy. In Sicily, the revolts of 1821 and 1848 and the landing of Garibaldi on the island's west coast in 1860 were events that involved the population more closely than in the relatively stable regions of northern Italy. Before 1812, Sicily had been united with Naples under Charles II of Bourbon in the Kingdom of the Two Sicilies. The revolution of 1812 was to have brought sweeping social changes of benefit to the *contadini*, as well as independence from Naples, but proved of short duration. The return to power of Napoleon, his defeat at Waterloo, and the principle of legitimacy proposed by the Congress of Vienna, resettled a monarch, Ferdinand I, on the throne of the Two Sicilies. So the old feudalism of Sicily returned unchallenged, and the social progress achieved by the 1812 constitution was undone before 1820.

The uprisings in Palermo and elsewhere in 1820 were the first step in the long struggle by the people against hardship and domination that was eventually to lead to the unification of Italy. In 1820, however, motives were far from clear; hopes for the reinstatement of the 1812 constitution mingled with dreams of Sicilian autonomy and better economic conditions for the peasants. From this point, in the 1820s—where Verga's great novel *Mastro-don Gesualdo* opens—there begins a forty-year period that the Sicilian novel has repeatedly illustrated.

The revolution of 1848 brought the island more in line with the European movement for freedom and democracy, and replaced the ideal of autonomy from Italy with that of unification with it in broad terms. The events of 1860 to 1862—Garibaldi's landing with his red-shirts, the plebiscite and the march on Rome—were rich with anti-climax. The idealism and patriotic fervour of those years were followed by a period of disillusionment and readjustment. This is the period of the *Risorgimento*, characterised by the cries of the dispossessed and the laments of the disappointed, that most fascinated the Sicilian novelist. In it he found an endless texture of rich human experience, a theatre of conflicts between that tradition-bound society just emerging socially from the Middle Ages, and the abruptness of changes in the social order precipitated by revolution and unification.

In the following discussion of the novels, three kinds of social change may be borne in mind: the passage from feudalism and conservatism to democracy and collectivism; agrarian reform, and the progress of education and cultural levels. Although not the only arbiters or indices of social change, these are certainly applicable to the *Risorgimento* in Sicily and the novels inspired by it.

GIOVANNI VERGA

Giovanni Verga occupies a special place in the history of Italian literature. He is usually associated with the theory of *verismo*, whose principles he set out in the famous letter to Salvatore Farina.[3] In this he declared his intention to write according to his observation of the real world: writing should record fact, be true to life and 'the hand of the artist will remain absolutely invisible'. This shows his attempt to give his work a kind of absolute objectivity; the facts of history must tell the tale and the author should not allow his standpoint or bias to intrude. Of course, it may be argued that the act of putting pen to paper is itself a subjective process, and that Verga's descriptions of peasant life in rural Sicily are informed by a deep compassion for the people's helplessness and the hardship they suffer. But this does not impair the *ideal* of objectivity, the artistic choice involved in an attempt to give his writing an internal logic and the illusion of truth.

It is certainly true that Verga's *Mastro-don Gesualdo* (first published in 1889) is rooted in the bitter historical realities of nineteenth-century Sicily, for the novel is at once the psychological history of one man and the picture of a whole society in transition. Its established position as one of the great novels of Italian literature is principally due to the artistic fusion of these two aspects. The first part of the novel identifies the motivations of

the character: an almost obsessive drive towards material better-
ment and the conviction of the efficacy of hard labour, Gesualdo
is seen as the successful peasant winning, against appalling odds,
the struggle to increase his personal wealth. Hated by peasant
and aristocrat alike, he is depicted through conversations and
description, a solitary figure animated only by his concern for
la roba, material possessions, which outweigh social, political and
even domestic considerations. In the interests of its political
usefulness he contracts marriage with Bianca Trao, daughter of
the local aristocratic family, spurning Diodata, the faithful representative of his own class.

The second part of the novel allows the character to fade back
into the mosaic of Gesualdo's society. The auction of communal
lands shows his victory over the various land-owning interests,
but the novel broadens out, touches lightly on the uprisings at
Vizzini and Palermo, and develops sub-plots in the episodes of
Nini Rubiera and the death of Don Diego Trao.

In its third section, the novel dwells on the story of Isabella,
Gesualdo's daughter, strengthening the theme of the incom-
patibility of classes (the marriage alliance) in a description of her
education which has reminded critics of Geltrude in Manzoni's
I Promessi sposi. The fourth and final section portrays the death
of Gesualdo and the failure of *la roba* to bring him fulfilment.
The religion of material possessions had made him betray his
origins in marriage; it had alienated him from his own family,
and from his daughter, whose language he does not speak. Thus
driven back into himself he finds no solace in a community which
envies him for his success, and solitude and death are his final
tragedy.

Gesualdo is a figure of gigantic proportions. Never far from
the surface of the novel, his psychology is drawn by description,
reports from minor characters and even by the countryside in
which he acts in a kind of sad harmony. In a sense, his very life
was the novelist's expression of important social realities, and his

success as an artistic creation, the feeling that he is fundamentally true to life, believable and impelling in historical terms—the aim of *verismo*—reflects Verga's concern for those realities.

The uprising of the 1820s had had little effect on the predominantly feudal nature of Sicily's economy and agriculture. Feudal control of land by aristocrats had been abolished from 1812 to 1825, but these laws had had little effect. The nineteenth century attempted to bring the whole apparatus of democratic collectivism to a region still labouring under the disadvantages of an entrenched feudal outlook. This is why Verga's novel shows the defects of the movement; it highlights the tragedy and pathos of a society thrust rudely into modern times. In 1820 the reforms brought about by the revolution gave Gesualdo the opportunity to outbid the barons at the public auction and take over their land. Sicilian agriculture had been organised according to the *latifondo* system. The landowner leased his land to middle men, who in turn leased it to the *contadino*, or labourer. Thus the enrichment of landowner and entrepreneur, and abject poverty for the *contadini*, was the inevitable result. Reforms were calculated to benefit the *contadini*, but *Mastro-don Gesualdo* is only one novel which shows how they simply allowed the more astute *contadino* to amass wealth at the expense of his fellows.

The revolution of 1848 proved a more serious threat to Gesualdo's growing empire, as it brought the redistribution of land and the apportioning of appropriate holdings to the *contadini* themselves. Gesualdo was now united with the barons in the common interest of self-preservation, and lent money to the peasants, knowing that, unprepared for the responsibilities of ownership and ignorant of agricultural methods, they would be unable to repay the loan and the land would return to him. All this provides the social fabric of the novel; the emotions and conflicts generated seem utterly *natural* through Verga's use, in his writing, of the idiom of the peasants. One of its greatest achievements is in the delineation of a social *type*, the individual who, through personal drive and initiative, capitalised on the reforming initiatives of his time and exploited them for personal gain. Again we should stress that Gesualdo is never a *type* in the artistic sense; rather, he is full to the brim with the fire and passion of personal ambition, softened by occasional touches of more conventional humanity (the scene after his marriage, compassion for Diodata etc).

The alliance with the Trao family provides another powerful indicator of social change that we shall meet again. Gesualdo's economic victory over the aristocracy was as complete as his domination of his fellow peasants. Yet, in spite of the attempt to remove the feudal yoke from the island by redistribution of land, Gesualdo's political marriage and his education of his daughter *as an aristocrat* betray a typically Sicilian cynicism about all change. If the aristocracy were to be powerless and penniless, why join them? Gesualdo's alliance reflects again the immunity of the island's long history to social change and the conviction that privilege in some form was an immutable fact of the region's destiny. Admittedly Verga's novels focus primarily on economic tragedy for the lower classes. However, *Mastro-don Gesualdo* was a literary character reflecting what really happened. Judging the winds of change and using them skilfully when they were blowing to his own advantage, he is a timeless symbol of exploitation and individual determinism. In that the novel depicts Sicilian agricultural society from 1820 to about 1860, it runs counter to the 'mythological' *Risorgimento*; it meditates on the harsher social realities that lie beneath all political change.

Similar themes emerge from Verga's other important novel, *I Malavoglia*, again concerning society in rural Sicily during the island's greatest trauma. In 1863 Padre 'Ntoni and his family are still the victims of the old economic system. The impact of the *Risorgimento* has been almost negligible on the society of Aci Trezza in the basic necessities of life, and the absolute solidity of the Sicilian family unit is symbolised in Padre 'Ntoni's stubborn refusal to contemplate any diversification in the family industry.

The loss of their boat, the *Provvidenza*, with its precious contents in a storm is responsible for the misery in which the family finds itself. Forced to accept loans from the moneylender, Campana di Legno, they sink deeper into debt and come more completely under his control. The picture of a society is again completely and faithfully observed, but here there is no principal giant character. As in the longer short story, *Pane Nero*, the central presence is family solidarity. When faced with the bitter realities of economic disaster, the family passes through every shade of despair and the conflicts generated are the fruit of the most acute psychological insights. Taken together, the novels become the single enduring Italian statement of the *Risorgimento*'s failure to reach the agricultural class. They demonstrate through a radical and important stylistic method the permanence of Italian social characteristics: the family in its concrete and impregnable formation, immune to changes in society of the most far-reaching kind, and the instinct for economic survival. At one end of the social scale at least, they also constitute a great artistic expression of the human comedy in Italian literature.

'ARISTOCRATIC' NOVELS

It has sometimes been observed that Verga is more accurate and compelling in the delineation of his peasants than of his aristocrats. There are several other novels which redress this balance, however, and contemplate the social effects of unification on other classes. Their very number testifies to the impact of the *Risorgimento* on the social fabric of the island and on the imagination of the novelist. 'Aristocratic' novels reflecting these effects range from Federico de Roberto's *I Vicerè*, first published in 1900; Luigi Pirandello's *I Vecchi e i giovani*, written during the period 1906–09, and Luigi Capuana's *Il Marchese di Roccaverdina*, published in 1901, to Giuseppe Tomasi di Lampedusa's *Il Gatto-*

pardo, published posthumously in 1958. All these novels, along with Giuseppe Maggiore's *Sette e mezzo*—a minor work, in artistic terms—reflect social changes in Sicilian society resulting from the momentous political events of nineteenth-century Italy.

FEDERICO DE ROBERTO

Federico de Roberto set his novel in Catania, Sicily, between about 1855 and 1882. He examines three generations of the aristocratic Uzeda family and the effect on them of the events of those years. In a vast tapestry of nineteenth-century Sicilian aristocratic life, De Roberto develops the theme that the *Risorgimento*, instead of breaking the power and influence of the aristocratic caste on the island, actually reinforced it. Like others of his generation, De Roberto had come under the spell of the naturalism of Zola and the *verismo* of Verga, but the attempt at psychological portraiture suffers, in literary terms, from the weight of his historical thesis. The characters and their setting provide a mosaic of contemporary life, but the book lacks the psychological penetration of a Mastro-don Gesualdo (the peasant), or Don Fabrizio (the aristocrat) in Lampedusa's *Il Gattopardo*. It seems that the unity is the historical thesis; and De Roberto's characters seem unable to escape from its stranglehold to assume lives of their own that are credible and real.

The motivations of the family are racism and money, both under attack in the new political situation. Its members demonstrate a pathetic attachment to the whole apparatus of pedigree and titles, and are naturally pre-occupied with the erosion of their economic power by the *Risorgimento*. This twin preoccupation motivates all the characters in varying degrees. Deprived by the institution of inheritance by the first-born, Don Blasco had become a monk, and is initially anti-*Risorgimento* when he sees that the take-over of Church lands will erode his leisured existence. He swiftly turns the situation to good account, however, buying up land and property for a song, and rapidly changes his affiliations to secure the results of this exploitation. Benedetto Giulente, the middle-class lawyer, aligns himself with the Red Shirts, but is soon disillusioned, deceived by manipulators and exploiters. After his election as mayor, his position changes very little as the real power has remained with the duke; and the candidature of Consalvo, the aristocratic cadet, for election as *deputato* in the Italian parliament, shows power flowing back inexorably into its former channels. Don Gaspare Uzeda, as the son who was not the first-born, has an interest in the *Risorgimento*, assuming a broadly liberal façade. Playing a double game, he secured election in a parody of the democratic process—the return of virtually feudal power to hands that had always held power.

Consalvo is by far the most interesting character. Growing up with the *Risorgimento*, he broadens his education by travel and, like Tancredi in *Il Gattopardo* and Goffredo in *Sette e mezzo*, shows the adaptability of the young aristocrat to the new social order. Consalvo was subject to influences both of upbringing and training, and also at an impressionable age to the idealism of revolution. He was thus able—by being born with a foot in both orders, so to speak—to harness his natural advantages in training for leadership in the new democratic order, retaining for his family its classic prestige and position. This phenomenon—a change of emphasis but, above all, adaptability to the new conditions—is dramatically powerful in all three novels by contrast. The older generation had lived too long in the old ways to adapt; they cannot relinquish feudal control for democratic power with any kind of dynamism; the Duca d'Oragua (*I Vicerè*), Don Fabrizio (*Il Gattopardo*) and Fabrizio Cortada (*Sette e mezzo*) are thrust sharply into dramatic contrast with this younger generation, showing in the novelists' imagination how social change at the level of real people becomes alienation of fathers from sons, and how social change generates far-reaching crises in that tightest of all social units, the Italian family.

I Vicerè is cyclic, then, in the sense that it charts the progress from the viceroys under the Bourbons to the new viceroy that Consalvo has become as president of the council. But, in its very completeness, the thesis—'All remains immutable'—is anti-historical. Certainly the novel reflects the disillusionment of many Sicilians with the *Risorgimento* with a good deal of pessimism—indeed, its atmosphere rings true—but it is not true that nothing changed. It seems that the historical thesis limits character, circumscribes the atmosphere of the book and, in the end, places an unnatural brake on naturalism.

LUIGI CAPUANA

Luigi Capuana wrote a psychological novel of crime and self-willed retribution in the image of Dostoyevsky—*Il Marchese di Roccaverdina*. Here the Sicily of the *Risorgimento* provides furniture and backcloth rather than central theme, for the author's concern is with his central character, and the context in which the marquis moves seems painted rather too faithfully in the colours of that psychology. In brief, the novel traces the successive stages in the gradual breakdown of the marquis's mind from the murder of his lover's husband to his final insanity. Everything is sacrificed to this end. The peasants, the countryside, the agrarian interests of the marquis, the dilettante antiquarian interests of Don Tindaro, and the important confession episode are changing scenes in a theatrical presentation of the psychology of remorse. Even the 'staged' recantation of the atheist Pergola, reflecting the shearing away of the last hope for the marquis of intellectual self-sufficiency, is a minor scene, sketched with rapidity, with its all too obvious significance for the protagonist.

Social change, then, is somewhat below the surface, but provided Capuana with a familiar setting. The story is set after 1860, and the marquis's family prestige has become an unconscious thing, felt instinctively as a duty, but no longer the fetish that the first generation of the Uzeda had created in *I Vicerè*. The marquis's brushes with the new social order show his objections to be material rather than of family pride. He plays a part in the formation of the new *Società agricola*, but here again the novelist is concerned more with the psychology of his protagonist than with social realism. Apart from the familiar values of a society polarised by extremes of wealth and customs, Capuana's theme seems to gain little from its immersion in a specifically Sicilian context and its positioning in time shortly after the Garibaldi landings.

GIUSEPPE TOMASI DI LAMPEDUSA

The most recent novel to dwell on the social change that the *Risorgimento* produced in Sicily has been Lampedusa's *Il Gattopardo*, published in 1958, which deals with the period 1860 to 1888, although its final chapter is a sequel, running on until 1910. At a distance of a hundred years, the theme has not lost its vitality; certain ironies in the compromise of the aristocrat with the new régime emerge in the light of this distance, for the author used the model of his great-grandfather on which to base the novel's protagonist, and the book is also a lament for lost things in the symbol of a family house destroyed by allied bombing in World War II. Anachronisms apart, *Il Gattopardo* centres on the life of Prince Fabrizio Salina, caught between the old system and the new—*a cavallo fra i vecchi tempi e i nuovi*—and forced to compromise with the new régime. The social conflicts we have been illustrating are dramatised with devastating effect in confrontations. Tancredi, the prince's nephew, espouses the Garibaldian cause, exhibiting just that adaptability we noted in Consalvo in *I Vicerè*, and distancing him—though not alienating him—from his uncle's inability to compromise. Fabrizio meets Chevalley, the representative of the Italian parliament, in a vivid contrast of the old and new ideals; he meets Don Calogero, the self-interested *nouveau riche* who is almost a Gesualdo figure, in a brilliantly ironic exposé of the principle of exploitation and social climbing; and, of course, Tancredi's union with Angelica, Calogero's daughter, completes the process of social transition in the second generation of *Risorgimento* Sicilians—the aristocrat has taken his place in the new Italy and the daughter of a peasant, through education, has risen to meet him.

These contrasts are dramatically realised through the novelist's technique of direct confrontation; the interviews of Chevalley and Calogero with Fabrizio are the novel's dramatic highlights. The prince is a leonine figure; his autocratic control of his family, detachment from the new political realities of his society, his interest in astronomy and his sceptical attitude towards the Church all build a powerful literary personality. Twin themes of love and death are woven into the fabric of the work, coming finally together in the chapter describing the Pantaleone Ball and the prince's death; to Fabrizio death appears as a woman dressed in brown, both seductive and the bringer of peace.

In spite of its standpoint—concerned, like other novels we have mentioned, with showing the *Risorgimento* in its true colours and painting its social effects on those caught up in it—*Il Gatto-pardo* illustrates the reality of social change following political change in a way *I Viceré* does not. For the novel moves on after the death of Fabrizio to show Angelica, risen to social accept-ability in her marriage to Tancredi, in another dramatically powerful confrontation with the aged Salina sisters in 1910. By now, the compromise has been made; the old régime—with its eloquent symbol, the stuffed dog Bendicò—is dead, and its descendants, the three spinsters, are shown pathetically dedicated to memories and superstition. But the aura of scepticism also encloses Angelica, no longer the captivating beauty, her marriage not the success of romantic literature, to show the author's final puncturing of *Risorgimento* idealism. The dictum that 'all must change so that things shall remain as they are' again rings the note of pessimism about the enduring effects of political and social change in their relationship with the immutability of human nature.

LUIGI PIRANDELLO

I Vecchi e i giovani, Pirandello's novel about this period stands somewhat apart from the others in that it describes the aftermath of disappointment and disillusionment with the *Risorgimento*. By the end of the nineteenth century the spirit of patriotic fervour which characterised the Garibaldi campaigns had faded. The birth of the Sicilian *Fasci*, or trade unions, between 1892 and 1894 might indeed have been seen as the logical outcome in socialism of some of the ideals of the *Risorgimento*.

The arrival of socialism in Sicily in 1891 had not been auspicious. The appeal of the *Fasci* to Sicilians had been economic rather than political or ideological, and the initial enthusiasm of the sulphur workers had depended on visions of material advantages. At once the old feudal machinery began to conflict with these unions, for the interests of landowners and middle-men alike were at stake. Gearing their procedure to the new political methods, they influenced their deputies, and in 1893-4, a bitter period of repression and brutality, the *Fasci* were suppressed. Pirandello's novel, like Verga's writing, illustrates the inability of the Sicilian *contadino* to cement into a new society the social advantages proposed for him by the *Risorgimento*. In the age-old traditions of a feudal society, the advantages of collectivism are swamped.

This was the political result of the *Risorgimento* described by one observer, Colajanni, in 1893 in a work that Pirandello used as a source.[4] In the novel itself the situation has predictable social results. The bitterness of those who could remember the idealism of 1848 and 1860, and who are forced to witness the repression of the *Fasci* and the Roman bank scandals, becomes a colour for the novel. The reactionary forces—landowner Flaminio Salvo, aristocrat Principe Ippolito Laurentano and the Church—are opposed by Crispi's envoy, Roberto Auriti, a son of the new Italy dispatched to Agrigento (Girgenti) to attempt reforms. This localised struggle, which documents the outworn values of *Risorgimento* patriotism, spreads to Rome, where the collapse of the banks seems to symbolise the collapse of the *Risorgimento* and its failure to create a new social and political system for modern Italy. The repression of the *Fasci* colours Pirandello's whole polemic with a deeper and more sinister pessimism. Stylistically, the novel breaks away from the Sicilian tradition we are describing in that the novelist's technique relies less on fundamental realities in Sicilian daily life. It is less concerned to show the lessons of the *Risorgimento* and its aftermath, linked with family life, domestic situations and the war of classes in compromise and adaptation. Examples in character delineation are Caterina Laurentano and Mauro Mortara—the first linked with the old world in her family and with the new in her life, and the mother of Roberto; the second, a kind of recluse living on memories of the glories of 1848 and 1860. These characters are more symbols of disappointment than human beings with a life of their own. Pirandello's standpoint of outrage at the failure of the *Risorgimento* to consolidate gains and build a new society overbalances the novel. It is a work of symbol and polemic rather than of plot and character, but shares with other examples of the literature of this theme the opposition to the myth of the unification of Italy as the foundation stone of a great and glorious modern Italy.

In a sense, the Sicilian novel of social change in the nineteenth century provides an antidote to official history; for without being documents in any complete sense, they document social results of political change. Invasion, participation and law become real life in the microcosm of the family, the context of career and the economic drive. The novel's broad canvas illustrates the full tones of these changes, but also the shadows and half tones; and it is in their breadth of treatment that the 'correction' element is introduced, for the legend of the *Risorgimento* was perhaps given a fresh dimension by the detailed scrutiny of the Italian current of nineteenth-century naturalism.

The constant return of the Sicilian novel to this theme and to the years 1820 to 1900, with two representatives in twentieth-century writing, also bears witness to the strength of the theme as an inspiration for novelists. The novelist's imagination was given free rein in the strong contrasts of class-confrontation, the aspirations of the *nouveaux riches*, and the clash of feudalism and collectivism. But looking more closely at the end of the century, we find other social changes mirrored in drama and the novel.

THE 'DRAMMA BORGHESE'

The drama of the middle class—from Giuseppe Giacosa's *Tristi amori* of 1887 to Pirandello's *Sei personaggi in cerca d'autore* of 1921 —reflects a society on which we have already commented. This was the generation of Chekhov, Ibsen and Strindberg; the time of the first impact of Freud and Einstein, and, in Italy, the heyday of D'Annunzio—that saw the end of a society of nineteenth-century values, of recognised principles, of God and patriotism, of man in charge and woman in the home. Italy from the 1880s to 1920s appeared to anticipate World War I in the disintegration of accepted values, particularly those of the middle class. That part of this movement, which can fairly be said to reflect social change—man in society, family and social context—we shall now discuss. The drama of Pirandello, although primarily centred on the Italian middle class, looks inside man himself (see Chapter 5).

With the drama of the *veristi borghesi*, or middle-class realists, we are close to social values powerfully present in Italian society today. Throughout the history of the peninsula the solidity and unity of the family as the fundamental unit of society has been important. Most Italians would agree that the family provides the co-ordinates of their immediate horizons. In it mingle the

Catholic consciousness of creation: its reverence for mothers of sons, the Latin jealousy and possessiveness of the male towards the female, and the conviction that business (commercial, domestic and private) is best conducted within the confines—however widely they are stretched—of that basic social unit. If a present-day Italian has a cousin in the motor trade, his car repairs will be done by this man; if his wife's sister-in-law is a hairdresser, hers will be the place to make an appointment. The centralisation of this process is partly due to geographical factors; Italians work and live in the same region on the whole, and regional affinities —reflecting the political position before 1860—are still strong.

Italian drama in the nineteenth century had transmitted those realities through the sieve of prevailing literary currents— romantic influences from France and the *verismo* of Verga. Verga's plays, and typically the best-known, *Cavalleria rusticana*, exhibit that uncompromising realism of his two great novels. The social values of a primitive Sicilian village, domestic betrayal, jealousy and ritual expiation through the duel are enduring facets of Italian—particularly Sicilian—primitive society, with echoes in today's concept of *omertà* (see p 170). Romantic comedies, on the other hand, tended to stereotype these social realities deriving from the family bond into love, tragedy and death; and we have to search hard for an Italian exponent—perhaps Paolo Ferrari in the footsteps of Dumas *fils*—of any other than historical significance.

But the drama of the middle class was to take another direction and to reflect social realism in a new sense. Social institutions were to be criticised or satirised; the industrial middle class was to import new values and new ethics; money earned and not money inherited became central. The life of this drama alternated between the office and the middle-class home; the wife's image varies between mother, homemaker and prestige possession. It is a drama of nine-to-five, of money and social standing, of pot plants in the window and church on Sundays. The principal exponents of this literary current in Italy were Giuseppe Giacosa and Roberto Bracco.

Seen against the background of permanent values in the context of the Italian family, which we have briefly described, the impact of middle-class realism can be measured. Imagine the first performance of Ibsen's *The Doll's House* or Strindberg's *Miss Julie* in front of an Italian audience of the late nineteenth century. Such an audience, with its unchallenged concept of family solidarity and family hierarchy, would have been profoundly disturbed to witness statements of the individual rights of woman in marriage outside the context of her husband's direct control. Giacosa proposed just this problem in *Diritti dell'anima*; Bracco deals with it in *Una Donna*, *L'Infedele* and in *Don Pietro Caruso*.

In *The Doll's House*, the wife was treated by her husband as a plaything or possession, and was denied intellectual independence. Her struggle to assert herself as an independent personality, leading to rejection of her husband when he finds himself unable to make this concession, provides the energy of Ibsen's play. In Roberto Bracco's *L'Infedele*, Clara is faced with a similar dilemma, but the problem has now become one of justification and faith; society accepted that the love of a husband should remain unquestioned yet imposed a duty on a wife to prove her love. A wife's love needs justification, but a husband's fidelity should not be questioned; this implicit double standard in his society is the target of Bracco's play.

To claim her right to the same trust that her husband, Silvio, enjoys, Clara had made a pact with him before the play opens: her fidelity was not to be questioned and, unquestioned, it would be guaranteed. Silvio, however, is a child of his time and cannot refrain from suspecting his wife in her relationship with Ricciardi, the third member of the triangle. Thus Silvio may have business friends, intellectual relationships and contacts with many people, while his wife may not without incurring suspicion.

Northern societies may find this dilemma has lost some of its force, but in Italian society the problem of a wife's independence in intellectual terms—excluding the modern possibility of her pursuing a profession—still invites active debate and touches an age-old nerve in many Italian men that is impervious to reason.

Giacosa examined substantially the same problem in his play, *Diritti dell'anima*. Again the balance of justice is finely set, and the theme of independence is repeated again and again in the *leitmotiv* of the wife's lament: 'Lo faccio perchè mi pare e mi piace' (I do it because I wish to and I want to). In the case of Bracco's play, *Una Donna*, the theme is extended into the field of sexual relations. Bracco gives an unusual twist to the question of sexual emancipation by showing the traditional roles reversed: Mario, the husband, clearly cannot provide for his family, while Clelia, his wife, may do so only if she is allowed by him to continue to exercise the oldest profession. Thus the strictures of society on individuals are placed in focus; the logical formula for survival of the family is taboo and the husband is the repository for these values. The play ends tragically with Clelia's suicide, but it lays bare many aspects of contemporary Italian society. Apart from the attitudes of the husband—demonstrating fully the traditional claustrophobic role of woman—there is the possibility of union in a child. The baby therefore deepens the colours of the play's comment on society, since Mario and his mother propose that it should be fostered.

In Bracco's *Don Pietro Caruso*, woman is again seen as the victim of a demanding society, and here the social conventions surrounding marriage are the target. Fabrizio, having violated Margherita, refuses to marry her, because he fears that the lowly condition of her father, Don Pietro Caruso, will damage his own elevated social standing. Two comments on contemporary society are immediately obvious: firstly, that the exaggeration of social stigma to the point where it could prevent marriage was still a factor in Italian society. But it should not be forgotten that this works both ways: Fabrizio would not marry her for reasons of social prejudice, nor would she continue to live with him— enjoying all the benefits of marriage—without society's official stamp. Both are caught up in a web of social prejudice whose effects are deepened, as before, when the father, Don Pietro Caruso, commits suicide. Secondly, the limited freedom of Margherita—her upbringing has been an education for enclosure rather than for liberty—is Caruso's lament at the end of the play.

Throughout these plays runs a strong current of social criticism, but they are never sermons. Bracco's raw material was the society in which he lived; his stage techniques and characters convey the emotions of real people. Abstract principles are perceived in comic and tragic aspects, therefore, scarcely ever abstracted from these portraits of woman at the mercy of a society in transition.

To gauge the distance Italian drama had moved towards a realistic portrayal of society and the scrutiny of principles on which that society was based in this generation, we might compare two plays whose central reality is adultery: Verga's *Cavalleria rusticana* and Giacosa's *Tristi amori*. From the start, Verga's classic play portrays values in a primitive society that are ageless and classless: jealousy, adultery, vendetta and expiation, and the Easter symbolism of the play sets it apart from the trivialities of middle-class social drama; but from the point of view of social change the comparison is instructive. Verga's Turiddu is the classic Sicilian of all time; returning to find his former fiancée attached to another, he cannot resist the temptation to make contact with her again, betraying the values of an ancient society. This betrayal causes challenge, duel and death in the highest artistic statement of the underlying realities of southern Italian society. Local custom and religious conscience combine to produce the inevitable framework of sin and expiation. The play has found a universal critical acclaim in that it portrays a social reality that has not changed for centuries.

Giacosa's play, *Tristi amori*, is set in a provincial Italian town. The husband Giulio finds that his wife Emma has been unfaithful to him with Fabrizio, his colleague; but there is no artistically logical dénouement in vendetta, the pistol shot or suicide. Giulio's reaction to adultery is more tragically intense in his decision to continue to live with his wife and their small daughter, Gemma. The more complex network of emotion and social values in middle-class society is painted in full colours. Just as the detailed exposition of Verga projects a primitive society complete in its setting, its details and its motivations, so Giacosa's *Tristi amori* is realistic as a portrait of middle-class society down to the tiniest detail. Verga's play was of 1883, while Giacosa's, with its totally different view of society and conclusion, was of 1887; between the two there are multiple contrasts: middle class and lower class, north and south, realism and verism, could be quoted. But both plays demonstrate the huge social differences in Italian society in the nineteenth century that we have hinted at already. Verga's Sicily remained virtually untouched by European social reform, the spirit of inquiry into the values of family life and northern movements towards a more open role for woman in society. Giacosa's Italy was showing just that spirit of inquiry by the 1880s in the meditations of her literature.

Bracco further discusses the children of a family in *Tragedia dell'anima* and *Maternità*, in an inevitable preoccupation with another fundamental principle in Italian society. Foreigners still wonder at the predominance of the children and their position of importance in the fabric of Italian family life; continuity of this family principle is often expressed in the well-known phrase '*buona fortuna e figli maschi*' ('Good luck and male sons'). Bracco's comment in *Tragedia dell'anima* is on the nineteenth-century Italian view that all rights concerning a child be with the father. The husband, Ludovico, finding that his wife's son is not his, attempts to separate her from her child, but Caterina refuses to contemplate this separation. The mother-and-child relationship is seen as a sacred and indissoluble bond in dramatic contrast to that between husband and wife. Typical of Bracco is the deepening of the tragedy when the child is found to have an incurable illness. Thus the traditional values of intimate relationships—husband-wife, mother-baby, wife-lover and father-son—are set in tragic conflict, producing a play of intense emotional power.

In his play, *Maternità*, Bracco poses the same problem, but utilises a wider range of dramatic devices. The emotions generated by maternity are conveyed through humour, by the stock theatrical device of a conversation overheard and in the many twists and turns of an involved plot which tends to be melodramatic. Again the principle of a woman's individual rights in marriage is stated, with the added poignancy of her refusal to tell her husband whether the baby is his. Through all Bracco's plays runs a passionate concern for the position of a wife in society and his conviction that she is often the victim of social prejudice, that she deserves the same intellectual rights as her husband and that children should be under her control rather than exclusively the prerogative of her husband.

When it is remembered that these plays were written almost a hundred years ago, and that such principles are still capable of arousing heated debate in present-day Italian society, their impact and modernity can be recognised. As a dramatic craftsman and as painter and critic of the values of his society, Bracco probably does not rank with Verga, Ibsen or Giacosa, but he deserves more consideration than hitherto as a dramatist of social change.

When we come to Giacosa's *Come le foglie*, of 1900, we are moving into the twentieth century in more ways than one, for the play documents the breaking up of the values of middle-class society in a way that looks forward to Moravia. Although the play is separated by nearly thirty years from Moravia's novel, *Gli Indifferenti*, the comparison is instructive in setting the works in their social context, for, in the framework of our theme, Giacosa stands for the close of the nineteenth century and Moravia for the *angst* of the twentieth century.

The plot of *Come le foglie* is fairly simple; the Rosani family is threatened by the dire consequences of poverty—just as Moravia's family was to be—and the way out is seen as a betrayal of accepted social values: the wife sells herself and the son becomes the lover of a rich woman whom he eventually marries. To this point the comparison with Moravia holds good on the surface; in *Gli Indifferenti*, the solution to poverty becomes the compromise of Carla with her mother's lover, Leo, involving Carla's brother Michele, who has the role of procurer thrust upon him. In his play, Giacosa injects a moralising note in the characters of Nennele and Massimo, jointly the middle-class ideal in the image of hard work and romantic love, which brings us back to Giacosa's generation and the ideals of Bracco. The corruption of middle-class ideals is shown in contrast with its antidote in the play, and critics from Croce on have seen this as a dilution of the play's authentic value. Massimo, particularly, embodies the ideal family man—stability and security—and his introduction into the play perhaps inserts too polemical a note. In spite of this, the two plays of Giacosa, *Tristi amori* and *Come le foglie*, convey the spirit of a generation—that gradual disintegration, transmitted through criticism, comment and satire, of the canons of behaviour within the social unit of the family in the nineteenth century. Unlike those of Roberto Bracco, Giacosa's plays are still popular today; their comments on Italian society in its more enduring aspects have lost little of their validity.

World War I marked a great dividing line in the history of the Italian people in the area of social change, just as it did for the literature of political conscience. While Moravia's famous novel mirrors the difficulties of the middle class under a Fascist-dominated society, so also, in a sense, do the plays of Pirandello. These reflections on twentieth-century society we shall examine in the concluding chapter, for—rather than the disintegration of society—they more accurately concern the dissection of man himself.

Social change has provided a resilient theme in Italian literature, particularly in modern times; and it was the broader spectrum of the play and the novel, or the artistic meditation on the human comedy from Boccaccio onwards, that supplied the outlets for this theme. From its more abstract preoccupations with religion and politics—man's destiny, meaning and organisation—literature looked downwards, as it were, to view his intimate preoccupation, his image, style, and family context. We have seen a society with such preoccupations in the Renaissance; the social results of decadence and the polarity of extremes in the eighteenth century, and the drama of the conflict of classes in nineteenth-century Sicily. On a slighter scale, we have mentioned the middle-class realism of Giacosa and Bracco, and their important links with the literature of present-day Italy. From all this literature of the Italian at home, there emerges a consciousness of a special life-style—changing down the centuries, but with its own specifically Italian preoccupations. The place of woman looms large; long repressed socially, she has often been the subject of the literature of social justice. The family unit with its concrete ideals of solidarity, maternity and continuity will perhaps survive longest in Italy. The conflicts of class—for long the artist's natural preserve in the juxtaposition of society's extremes—still haunts a society divided between industrial aristocracy and a repressed agricultural class. The concern with style—the Italian's natural aesthetic sense transferred to his own context—has always added flavour and colour to the Italian literature of social change.

Notes to this chapter are on p 176

CHAPTER 4

The Catholic Conscience

As with the other themes of Italian literature, that reflecting the
Catholic conscience has constituted a rich vein. The distinction
should be made at once between literature reflecting a religious
view of the world, with which we are here concerned, and the
'religious literature' of sermons, doctrinal works, hagiography
and that body of Italian writing whose intentions and results are
specifically religious. The latter type has come to be known in
Italian as *letteratura religiosa* or *letteratura di pietà*, and its aspirations are consistent with those of the Church, primarily fulfilling
the needs of the faithful.[1] In the present context, we are concerned
with works of literature whose aims may well have been persuasive,
to edify and to teach, but of which the results have received
critical acclaim as literary works. The two greatest examples, by
Dante and Manzoni, are certainly not considered as *letteratura
religiosa* today, but rather as valid meditations on the human
condition with a religious *theme*. This is what we mean by the
Catholic conscience in Italian literature.

The theme was at its most potent at moments of religious
revival, crisis and change in the history of the peninsula. We
shall here consider the literature of the Catholic conscience after
Dante at two important moments—the Counter-Reformation
with Torquato Tasso, and the *Risorgimento* with Alessandro

Manzoni—with some comment also on the theme before Dante and its manifestations after 1870.

The Italian Catholic today may look back over some seven centuries during which two realities have been virtually constant: Italy has been the home of the Catholic religion, its centre in the Roman papacy, and, as a Catholic, the Italian is in a majority compared with all other sects. In other words, to a greater degree perhaps than in any other Christian country, the Church and her fortunes have been closely integrated with national life and there are more Catholics than dissenters. These twin strengths have had their effects on the literature of the Catholic conscience—not always a beneficial effect, in the eyes of some critics—but the Catholic view of life in all its aspects is as Italian as *pasta* and *parmigiano*. As with the literature of the political conscience, the theme thrived best on aggression; Catholic crisis and change are not far removed in time from the greatest literature of the Catholic conscience. The need for spiritual renewal informs the work of Dante; self-examination and doubt, the work of Tasso, and the impetus towards a hitherto undreamed-of separation of Church and state had already begun when Manzoni published *I Promessi sposi*. As with politics, so with religion. The peace and calm of settled relationships hardly provided the conditions in which great literature was to flourish. In Italy Catholics have never suffered the consequences of being in a minority and not until comparatively recent times has the Church been denied her classic control over many aspects of the everyday lives of Italians.

For the origins of that fusion of ecclesiastical and historical destinies we must return to the Middle Ages; the interpenetration of religion and life in Italy was more complete in the twelfth and thirteenth centuries than at any time since. Religion played a part in the flowering of Gothic architecture, the establishment of universities, the tradition of chivalry and the development of representative institutions. It was also a fundamental influence on the rise of vernacular literature and the creation of new types of religious orders; and, as these two come together in St Francis, this should be our starting point.

ST FRANCIS

The characteristics of the new spirituality of the thirteenth century were mysticism and a return to primitive origins in the—primarily—Franciscan ideal. The Catholic religion became more intimately involved with social issues. St Francis founded the famous mendicant order in Assisi in 1206, dedicated to poverty, humility, penitence, charity towards one's neighbour and total submission to the will of God. This ideal—the conviction that Christians should leave the abstract meditations of monasticism and immerse themselves in the everyday world, devoting themselves to charitable social service—has remained a significant current in all Italian literature and has often contrasted with the more abstract, doctrinal and hierarchical aspects of Church organisation represented by the papacy. Indeed, the modern politico-religious theme of Silone's *Avventura di un povero cristiano* looked back to precisely this contrast of religious ideals at the beginning of Italian literature (Celestine V and Boniface VIII). Poverty and charity, the twin themes of the Franciscan campaign, inform the literature of the Italians from St Francis and Jacopone da Todi to Dante. It was as necessary to enter the field of political and social life to infuse the new civilisation with a genuinely evangelical spirit, as it was to bring Christian ideals to the wider group of Italians through the spoken tongue.

Thus the *Cantico di Frate Sole* of St Francis is a literary work of dual importance for us here. In a sense, it was a full statement of the Franciscan ideal, initiating an important theme for Italian literature; and it was written in Italian, in which language it was the first major work of significance for all Italians. The greatest works of literature to use the Catholic theme are never far from the Franciscan ideal. In Manzoni's great novel, for instance, it is precisely the ideals of poverty, charity and evangelism that provide a spur for characters such as Fra Cristoforo, Federico Borromeo and, ultimately, *L'Innominato*.

The *Cantico* is a simple hymn of praise. It thanks the creator for all the benefits of creation, both great and small, in an atmosphere of peaceful harmony and fraternal relationships. Its force is due to the totality of its vision; love and humility go hand in hand, and the poet embraces the whole world in an aura of trust and friendship. Sin and death emerge only as natural constituents of the all-pervading beatific vision.

JACOPONE DA TODI

In stark contrast, the *Laude* of the Umbrian Jacopone da Todi dwell on the unworthiness of man and his physical corruption. Like St Francis, Jacopone had devoted himself to religion after a personal crisis, but his writing constitutes both a continuation of Franciscan ideals and their opposite or mirror image. Evidence of Franciscan joy in the unity of man with God is rare; far more common are Jacopone's delineations of human vices, the vanity of the things of this world and satire of contemporary customs.

A legend of mystery and horror surrounds the figure of Jacopone, associated as he was with the Flagellant movement, in his conviction that man must rid himself through punishment and penance of all vices, reducing himself to abject humility before being considered worthy of divine love. In the work of St Francis, the world in all its imperfection is embraced in a spirit of brotherly love; in the *Laude* of Jacopone, its corruption is painted in all its horror.

DANTE ALIGHIERI

The Italian Catholic conscience was to find its most enduring expression in Dante, of course, in that consummate synthesis of the great themes of Italian literature seen in the *Divine Comedy*. We must not limit Dante to the strictures of the Catholic theme, for we have seen that he is as political and social a writer as any representing those themes; but the standpoint of the *Comedy* is a notable advance on St Francis and Jacopone. Dante's supreme advantage was organisation. If the spoken language as a vehicle for literature was born in St Francis, Italian literary *form* was born in the *Divine Comedy*; for the whole apparatus of medieval catholicism—hierarchical and doctrinal, monastic and Franciscan, love and charity with justice and order—was poured into the single intellectual mould. So, with Dante, the place of religion in Italian life—in ideal collaboration with the world of government and organisation of his time—finds a prophetic position because the *Comedy* contains not only a synthesis of renewed and revitalised Christianity, the legacy of the thirteenth century, but also the announcement of cracks in the edifice that Italians were to suffer down the centuries.

It has been said that the *Divine Comedy* 'is at once the extreme literary expression of the medieval synthesis [of religion and culture] and a prophetic denunciation of the apostasy of Christendom'.[2] That prophecy is the history of the Italian Catholic, which is not our present preoccupation, but its manifestations in Italian literature reflect the truth that religion and society, Church and state, were never again to find such a fruitful union and collaboration. Some of the success of the *Divine Comedy* is doubtless due to its breadth of vision—taking in the vision of a St Francis, the consciousness of human imperfection of a Jacopone and an encyclopedic range of the whole spectrum of medieval Catholic life.

By the time of the Italian Renaissance, the evidence of very great literature had become almost the example of this fusion and the symbol of a lost greatness. The Church had lived on in the present and prophetic corruption that Dante had described; the new intellectual exigencies of the birth of humanism seemed to demand a better Church than that symbolised by Renaissance popes and the practices of the Roman *curia*. The explosion of art and letters in the late fifteenth and early sixteenth centuries seemed to leave the ancient edifice of the Roman Catholic Church far behind. Popes were patrons, but scarcely spiritual leaders to rank with the greatest; the materialism of commerce and the imperialism of conquest animated and occupied the officials of the Church, partly due to the problems of the territorial papal state and the threat to Christian Europe from the Turk. Then came Luther—a new threat was posed to the fabric of the Roman Catholic Church; already concerned with reform among its more energetic and feeling members, it now needed to compete with the spreading gospel of personal faith, lay participation and reformed liturgy. We should not forget that the Protestant Reformation could have heralded invasion and conquest in the Italian Renaissance mind. It must have seemed to many that the unity of religion and culture had been broken for ever.

THE COUNTER-REFORMATION

The greatest literary flowering of the Counter-Reformation period—Torquato Tasso's *Gerusalemme liberata*—was a tortured attempt at re-uniting them. As the work typifies the attempt by catholicism to re-harness to its own chariot the greatest intellectual and artistic achievements of the Renaissance, we should take a brief look at the period. The sack of Rome by German troops in 1527 was seen by contemporaries as a divine judgement on the division and corruption of the Church, and hopes for rejuvenation were pinned on the idea of a general council. Many hoped also for a return to the Christian unity of the *trecento*—a rebirth, perhaps, of Dante's ideal of a Christian society where once more empire and Church would constitute the old harmony and the centre of the world would be Italy.

This was not to happen, however. In spite of early attempts at

reform—the Lateran Council called by Pope Leo X; the con-
ciliatory efforts of the Venetian cardinal, Gasparo Contarini, and
a genuinely new 'Franciscan' activity in the shape of the *Compagnia
del divino amore* (1497), an order devoted to charitable activities—
these initiatives failed to keep pace with the growth of Protestantism. In the 1530s, hopes for Catholic rejuvenation ran high; Pope
Paul III welcomed reform, made the main reformers cardinals,
and initiated a charter of reforming plans called the *Consilium de
emendenda ecclesia* (1537). The 1540s set the seal on the rest of the
century in a spirit of aggression rather than conciliation. The
conference of Catholics and Protestants at Regensburg failed to
agree; Paul IV ascended the papal throne, and the institution of
the Holy Office, or Inquisition, showed the teeth of the Catholic
Reformation. Finally the Councils of the Church, between 1545
and 1563, gradually codified principles and practice, excluding
Protestants from its sphere and laying the bases of the Catholic
religion for generations of Italians to come.

TORQUATO TASSO

By an accident of history Torquato Tasso and Carlo Borromeo—
the dedicated cardinal-reformer of Milan—were almost exact
contemporaries. Borromeo typifies post-Tridentine catholicism in
the driving energy of reform and a rigidly hierarchical view of the
organisation of the Church. He stands, perhaps, for both its best
and worst aspects. Tasso represents, in the many twists and turns
of a troubled life, the crisis of the intellectual during the Counter-
Reformation. The Renaissance Italian writer, complete with his
baggage of classical and humanistic experience (and the living
epic tradition from Pulci to Ariosto) was now faced with a duty to
be serious. Like Alessandro Manzoni so much later, the literary
qualities of his great work may have brought critical acclaim in
spite of, rather than because of, this seriousness; for the artist of
the late sixteenth century was subject to duties and restraints that

had scarcely hampered Raphael and Ariosto, artists of the High Renaissance. The Inquisition censored the work of the Venetian painter, Paolo Veronese; the Council of Trent had approved the Index of proscribed books; Giordano Bruno was to die at the stake, and an artist like Michelangelo, living through both generations, so to speak, was wracked by doubts and crises of faith in his last years.

Tasso's *Gerusalemme liberata* is the poetic statement *par excellence* of the Catholic conscience of those years—the translation, in as far as it was to be possible, of Renaissance idioms into the language of the new conscience. 'Conscience-stricken' perhaps describes that society more accurately, for in its main emphasis the work has moved away from that liberty of free expression, the jostling of magic, chivalry, love and wide-eyed delight that characterised Ariosto's *Orlando furioso*. The *Gerusalemme liberata* is a poem of the First Crusade, of sober war, of right and might harmoniously united in the struggle for a new Christian society. Its central theme is the siege and conquest of Jerusalem—in the hands of the Saracens—by the Christian Goffredo di Buglione, but its huge tapestry is woven in a rich variety of themes which owe much to the epic example of the *Iliad* and the *Aeneid*, as well as the more recent Italian epic tradition culminating in Ariosto's *Orlando furioso*.

The Christian theme of the Crusade, therefore, permitted Tasso to combine the new ideal of Christian achievement with the themes of love, nature and military endeavour that were traditional in the Italian epic genre. The historical framework, based on the events of 1096-9, utilised events that were set far enough back in the past to allow him freedom to adapt and elaborate his material to suit sixteenth-century needs and to permit the inclusion of supernatural elements: the intervention of the angels on the side of Christians and demoniacal forces on the side of Saracens. But, in the context of our present theme, Tasso's poem may be seen as an accurate register of the religious conscience of his time without denying the validity—or indeed superiority in artistic terms—of the theme of love stemming from classical and Renaissance models, the enjoyment of the theme of war and the literary use of the natural background. Although important in the *Gerusalemme liberata*, these themes are overlaid with a new sensibility, a feeling for them which is a product of the poet's own troubled life and the troubled conscience of his times.

The period of gestation of the poem, 1559–75, represents the consolidation of the Counter-Reformation. Spanning the peace of Cateau-Cambrésis and the Roman Jubilee of 1575, when bishops reported to their master in Rome on the progress of the Tridentine reforms in their dioceses, the period could count various successes for the new Catholic life. First among these was the victory of Christian over Turk at Lepanto in 1571, and the parallel with the theme of the Crusade in the poem is obvious. Then the Council of Trent finished its work in 1563, reaching various conclusions of importance for writers. The Index was to submit their works to the scrutiny of moral and religious conformity, and that other arbiter, the Inquisition, could already use their writings as indicators of orthodoxy. The New Orders—St Ignatius and the *Exercises*, for instance—had an undeniable influence on the growing importance, for Catholics as well as Protestants, of individual conscience, and the necessity for internal and personal reform.

This is the background to Tasso's generation, but he was also a troubled individual; the artistic success of his poem was in strong contrast with the personal failure of his life. His personal tragedies were constant dissatisfaction with his various masters in the world of court patronage, inherited from Ariosto, on which he was to depend throughout his life; a readiness to take offence; continuing war with piratical printers of his works, and intermittent ill-health that periodically affected the stability of his mind. All these misfortunes, with others, domestic and financial, were crowned by his imprisonment between 1579 and 1586.

Seriously devoted to religion, he yet needed constant reassurance, refusing to allow his troubled conscience to be appeased by inquisitorial examination of his orthodoxy.

While the events of his life and the religious climate of his times do not alone account for Tasso's Catholic conscience in the *Gerusalemme liberata*, they do help us to understand it. Artistically, the critic has a duty to judge the extent of the success of this marriage between the epic ideal—love, arms and nature in Ariosto's formula—and the Counter-Reformation ideal of reformed Christian conscience and practice.

Two themes of Tasso's religious inspiration can be identified here and, in a sense, contrasted, although they represent complementary aspects of contemporary Christianity. The first theme is almost a mystic preoccupation with man's failure to communicate with God—a crisis of personal faith, perhaps, in the poet himself, which recalls Michelangelo in his last years. Characteristic of the end of the sixteenth century, the theme represents the Counter-Reformation necessity for internal renewal, is reflected in the personal crusade of the saints of the period and has a flavour of Jacopone rather than St Francis. The second theme is the formal and outward aspect of Counter-Reformation catholicism: the enjoyment of ceremony and liturgy, pomp and processions and, in contrast with the first theme, the comfort of secure and certain repose for the Christian soul in the bosom of the Church. Here we have another important side of religious life in Tasso's lifetime. The exterior forms of Italian catholicism—art and architecture on one hand, and music and liturgy on the other —had been considered and re-ordered by the Council of Trent. Churches were to be repaired and decorously ornamented in accordance with a proper respect for the House of God; the *Canons and Decrees* of the Council had laid down what was to remain and what was to go in church ceremonies. This latter theme surfaces in the poem to add little to its force. The theme is concerned far more with the poem's furniture, a dignity and gravity of detail whose intention was to bring the poem into line with the Church's reformed practice and avoid censure by the Inquisition.

So for literature, the first religious theme was an advantage, the second a disadvantage. The isolation of the individual religious conscience and a striving after unfulfilled ideals brought a psychological penetration that we do not find in Ariosto's *Orlando furioso*; the 'furniture' of religious ceremony, processions and sermons clutter the poem with descriptions irrelevant to the main action, often diluting its impact. One episode will serve to illustrate the contrast, though it is perhaps indicative of an important truth—that this particular dualism of religious inspiration in the poem (and the difficulty of reconciling these two aspects artistically) is the dualism of the poet himself and a dualism in the lives of many Italian Catholics in the sixteenth century, from Gasparo Contarini at the beginning of the century to Giordano Bruno at the end. The dualism is the search for a personal religious faith and the corporateness, and duty to conform, of Catholicism. The first was an important constituent in Protestantism *and* Catholicism—at any rate until the 1540s; and the second was the rationale of hierarchy and obedience that characterised post-Tridentine Italy. The warmth of a personal relationship with God contrasts with the cold comfort of religious forms. Of course, it is easy for a Protestant sensibility to place side by side two extremes of the same spectrum for deliberate effect, and the effect is artificial. But we are here concerned with the artistic reconciliation of apparently contrasting aspects of religious conscience in the poem. In the totality of his vision, Tasso's religious inspiration provides a microcosm of the sensibility of the Counter-Reformation.

Let us examine one episode, then, to see the relationship between poetry and Counter-Reformation catholicism. The two themes come together in the spiritual awakening of Tancredi after he discovers he has killed Clorinda. Her dying request for baptism is a personal religious experience, perhaps, but this is followed by the admonition to return to the Crusade (from which Tancredi has been distracted by the love of a pagan woman) by Peter the Hermit.[3] The death of Clorinda at Tancredi's hand introduces the theme of conversion, so that the end result of the chivalric duel is baptism rather than simply honour. So the themes of love, chivalry and war (with the figure of an Ariostesque warrior-woman an adjunct) mingle with evangelism. The combined emotional effect of Tancredi's recognition of Clorinda and her conversion provides a passage of lyrical delicacy (in lines 66–71). All the traditional elements are present in the episode, but its climax—the sense of wonderment and inadequacy, the personal religious experience of Tancredi—reflects much that is recognisable in the Counter-Reformation sensibility. We might associate this individual religious fulfilment with all the 'private' workers for a better Christian life, in the monasteries, in the streets, and with the missionary zeal of the Church abroad. The sermon by Peter the Hermit (85–9) which follows this experience in the poem has been seen as breaking the spell woven by Tasso in the episode. It is an exhortation to return to the Crusade, forsaken for love of a pagan, couched in terms of stern admonition. Is this the figure of the Inquisitor looming in the background? Is it Tasso's own deep-felt feeling of spiritual inadequacy? Certainly, the sermon lacks the poetry, the fire of love, the tears of death and emotional strength of the Tancredi-Clorinda encounter. But, of course, this is right. Peter the Hermit represents the Church, or duty, or conscience, or all three. His admonition represents the Catholic need for discipline and the sense of certainty in established procedure conveyed by the official authority of the Church. While the poetic temper varies noticeably, the two episodes complement each other in a composite picture of the spirituality and discipline of the Counter-Reformation, dual facets of the poet's complex personality, probably, and an entirely logical juxtaposition of two facets of contemporary religious experience. It is the totality of the poet's vision that gives the *Gerusalemme liberata* one of its strengths.

So the epic has lost some of its magic, the laughter and the irony in its passage from Ariosto to Tasso. The colours of the poem are deepened, not brightened; in the *Gerusalemme liberata*, war and carnage are not treated with Ariosto's restraint. But love is fully explored, in spite of Tasso's soberer intentions, in a marvellous blend of the sensuous and the natural, and even becomes more mature in the depiction of yearning and frustration, a psychological rather than surface description which looks forward to the Romantics. The love between Sofronia and Olindo, Tancredi and Clorinda, Erminia and Tancredi, Rinaldo and Armida is created in a spirit of free inquiry. Love is often unfulfilled or frustrated, rarely restrained by moral censure.

With a poem of such vast dimensions it would be possible to show by many examples how Tasso's Renaissance heritage, both classical and vernacular, was adapted to the Catholic conscience of his times.[4] The one example we have discussed brought together contrasting but complementary aspects; others could show Ariosto's legacy spoiled and disordered in poetic terms. There is no doubt, however, that the poem's unity of inspiration, its intimate life and feeling, its eclectic but accomplished technique, qualify it as one of the greatest literary manifestations of the Italian Catholic conscience.

ALESSANDRO MANZONI

It is difficult to restrict the greatest works of literature to their predominant themes or their historical circumstances. Dante and Tasso registered the Italian Catholic conscience at important moments in time, but seem infinitely larger than those moments. Manzoni's masterpiece, the historical novel, *I Promessi sposi*, reflects this conscience at an important time, but outlives that conscience and that time to become a part of the make-up of every cultured Italian. Schoolboys obliged to learn by heart Manzoni's famous description of Lake Como, commentators on the language of Italian literature drawn back to Manzoni's formulation of it in the novel, even modern viewers of a recent television serialisation of the work are all part of the same process—the continuing and living absorption of a great work into the national personality.

Manzoni's novel has had this effect on the literary and cultural history of Italy, so much of what we today recognise as the essence of Italian culture, the spirit of the Italian people, has roots and reflections in its pages. A reading of the novel is, in one sense, an introduction to modern Italy—a foreshadowing of many of her problems, social, political and moral—and, in another, a statement of her character just before the irreversible changes of the *Risorgimento* took place (see p 106). This is why the siting of the novel as a work of the Catholic conscience is so dangerous, it is so much more than that.

The period 1821–7, which saw the gestation of *I Promessi sposi*, falls between two events of prime importance for modern Italy: the French Revolution and the revolution of 1848. The novel was actually produced, therefore, between the collapse of the old world and a significant affirmation of the new, with its roots in the illuminist traditions of the eighteenth century and portents for the *Risorgimento*. This is to view it in political terms, however, for the work is also a great consolidation of linguistic theories about the Italian language in art, the modern analogue, in this sense, of the *Divine Comedy*. Again, this is still not enough. Manzoni's literary environment was European Romanticism, and he was in the thick of the debates centred in Milan between Italian and French men of letters. Finally, the novel projects the Catholic conscience as an inspiration and moving force for literature firmly into modern times, for the Manzonian formula of social values—an equation of oppressors and oppressed, good and evil characters in conflict in society—now extends to involve humble folk. There was no place for Renzo and Lucia in literature before the nineteenth century; Dante and Tasso had worked with characters and within frameworks whose limits were defined by what was appropriate for literature; Manzoni and, later, Verga were innovators in this specific sense: they brought believable ordinary people within the range of the novel form, and the novel form within the range of the ordinary reader. Importantly, Manzoni's vision was moral and Catholic, reflecting the great nineteenth-century attempt at that unity of religion and life we have been describing.

The event in Manzoni's life of crucial importance for his novel was his conversion to Catholicism in 1810. From this point his total vision of the world and its history changed. Manzoni devoted the rest of his life to a working out of his own particular version of that unity, the fundamental concept of the role of providence and God in history, society, politics and the dilemma of the individual. His *Inni Sacri* were the first fruits of that inquiry into the relationship between catholicism and the world; *I Promessi sposi* was its artistic consummation. Between these two poles stand the *Conte di Carmagnola*, a historical tragedy, and the *Osservazioni sulla morale cattolica*. In the first he examines the relationship between the individual and an unjust society—almost a microcosm of the great world of the novel—in a historical context. In the second, he lays the theoretical basis and foundation for the scale of values and Catholic conscience that was to emerge fully formed in his masterpiece.

Thus the conversion of Manzoni provided him with the impetus to see the world in a new light; the *Osservazioni* were the working out of a coherent system of relationships between faith and experience; and the *Promessi sposi* is the artistic fulfilment of these elements. Faith and morals, perhaps dry subjects by themselves, are inserted into history and society; good and evil are fused with the more common motivations of society, material aggrandisement and honour; while the canvas on which these struggles were depicted grows to the dimensions of a whole society. Figures of historical and political significance mingle with recognisable Italian peasants; the forces of history, war, corruption, plague, revolution and famine mingle with those more abstract forces of conscience—sanctity and self-sacrifice—and the latter do not dominate the former in the novel's artistic balance. The play of forces on characters is accomplished with realism inviting credibility and with a completeness that has defied imitation. The novel has a unity found only in the greatest works.

The tools of Manzoni's Catholic vision are history and realism. History provides the framework in which his characters move. The story of the poor lovers, Renzo and Lucia, is set against a background of closely documented historical fact—the society of the first quarter of the seventeenth century—using the fiction of the author's discovery of a contemporary manuscript. So the method of history was also a concern for realism, for what is true, what is fact. The politics of Spanish Milan, the figure of Cardinal Federico Borromeo, the bread riots and the plague are all researched portraits of historical accuracy. In these contexts move the characters, again meditated and developed with psychological insight. Thus Manzoni has powerfully persuasive arguments further to convince the reader that, given context and psychology, *motivation* also is natural, according to the random dictates of human nature rather than in accordance with some pre-ordained moral scheme. Renzo and Lucia live through the trials of love, a pure and timeless sentiment, frustrated by evil ambition (Don Rodrigo) and weakness (Don Abbondio) as well as bureaucratic corruption (Azzeccagarbugli). The play of good and evil forces reaches its dramatic climax in the conversion of *L'Innominato*, upon which the tide turns. Aided by hope, Christian fortitude and providence, the lovers are finally rewarded by their union.

The history and symbolism are not simply a treatise and a sermon. Motivation rarely seems imposed on a character by his author's moral conscience; rather motivation is endemic to character and situation. The historical background and the moral motivations provide credible characterisation in human terms; the laws of God are fused with the weaknesses of human nature in a concrete artistic edifice. History provides a background against which characters and their moral choice seem to move naturally. So the wanderings of Renzo are not simply a digression but constitute a progress towards his own maturity and self-awareness, a purgatory whose darkest hour is his drunkenness at the inn. The vacillating Don Abbondio is an intensely believable portrait of moral weakness in the face of adverse circumstances. He represents every priest, providing the artistic measure of the sanctity of Borromeo through his readily recognisable humanity. The episode of Geltrude, the Nun of Monza, is not only a detailed condemnation of a contemporary ecclesiastical institution, but also an artistic foil for the steadfastness of Lucia. Many examples could be cited. One of the great strengths of Manzoni's novel was a fusion of motivation, informed at every turn by the values of catholicism, with the processes of art, with character, situation, psychology and history. Perhaps this is why the work will continue to entertain where it no longer edifies.

Of course, there were multiple dangers in the attempt to create a believable artistic work from the moral dilemma. The reader must decide for himself whether characters live and move apart from their particular situation in the moral struggle; whether history constitutes digression; whether action and pace are hindered by these episodes, and whether the victory of the good is psychologically prepared rather than simply morally appropriate. Possibly today the results seem more important than the intention; and we should not forget that the 'moral symbolism' is not always as simple as it looks: in characters like Don Abbondio and Fra Cristoforo the struggle between good and evil takes place within man. Even if Lucia seems a paragon of maiden virtues at times, is not this a part of the translation into art of the moral dilemma? Her constancy balances Renzo's waywardness, her timidity his courage; her principles balance the images created by Manzoni for his other female characters, Geltrude, Agnese and Perpetua. These latter are more believable, but then so is Fra Cristoforo more immediately recognisable than Borromeo. The characters are part of Manzoni's moral spectrum, a wide range of individuals all affected by the necessity of individual choice, but living and breathing in historical situations individual to them.

What, then, was the Catholic conscience for Manzoni? Summarising, it is a currency of thought and motivation that informs all the characters; it places them individually in a position to choose between the corrupt uses of the world and the truths of the Catholic religion, and documents their choice in a way that is psychologically convincing. Don Abbondio's conscience is a theatre of war between the knowledge that it was right and just to marry Renzo and Lucia and the fear of worldly reprisal; Renzo is impelled by a sentiment of pure love, but will have to overcome unchristian over-reaction to corruption until, chastened, he will have his reward; Fra Cristoforo will overcome a naturally belligerent temperament to 'atone' for past sins in religious service; and *L'Innominato* rises higher in the moral spectrum than any other character from a starting point lower than anyone, providing the dramatic climax of the moral struggle and the turning point in the novel's story. Thus Manzoni's characters never really teach; they are products of their age, fight their individual moral battles in terms of their historical circumstances, each according to his place in a kind of Noah's Ark of seventeenth-century society.

If it was Manzoni's achievement to make his humble and ordinary characters as believable as those, like Borromeo, who had had a life before the novel, it may also be appropriate to see his achievements in the Italian language in this light. For, if the grace of God was universally available to all Manzoni's characters, then the novel of its acceptance or rejection should be available to all, readable in a language common or comprehensible to all. The language of *I Promessi sposi*, based on the author's close study, became popular, natural and realistically Italian, particularly in the novel's final revised edition. Foreign influences and the dialect of Lombardy were finally abandoned in favour of Florentine, modified according to the canons of use.

It is almost impossible to turn back the clock in an attempt to visualise the effect of *I Promessi sposi* on its first readers. Without warning, Italian literature had abandoned the formalisms, poetic language and all the high-flown principles of eighteenth-century art. Suddenly, the novel emerged into and became part of Italian society. The people were recognisable; they spoke the language of every day; they suffered from oppression just as the Lombards were suffering under Austria, and most importantly the Catholic conscience—a fundamental current in all Italian societies—now provided the driving force of a great modern novel. Today, that conscience finds other directions, no less important as a constituent of the national consciousness, but in Manzoni's writing it found a literary expression in the conviction of a Catholic writer, strengthened by the immediacy of conversion and supported by the intellectual stimulus of dedicated study. This is why *I Promessi sposi* is a national monument in Italy. It is simply so Italian. Apart from its influence on the modern Italian literary language, it expressed the values of every nineteenth-century Italian household; it saw those values in a defined historical context. No other novel so accurately reflects the Catholic conscience in Italian society at one point in time, and no other is so universal in the resonance it finds with the Italian Catholic conscience in all time.

Of course, a work whose driving force is the principles of the Catholic religion can never completely please those whose beliefs lie elsewhere. Moravia acutely observed that one of the secrets of the book's impact on its first readership was the fact that they were more Catholic than subsequent generations. The artistic co-ordinates of the novel are indeed 'the ideological framework of Catholicism', and it is also true in a sense that 'Catholicism then, for the last time, informed all Italian life'.[5] We may see why the Catholic conscience has become no longer a dominant theme for great literature after Manzoni by examining two further works: *Le Mie prigioni* of Silvio Pellico and *Il Piccolo mondo antico* of Antonio Fogazzaro.

SILVIO PELLICO

From our examination of the Italian political conscience it will be remembered that Pellico, a contemporary of Manzoni and sharing his romantic origins, had brought together the political and religious themes in his most famous work (see p 66). Moving on to that fateful generation after Manzoni which witnessed the events in the second half of the nineteenth century, we find a similar conjunction of themes in Fogazzaro's *Il Piccolo mondo antico*. Both works are novels of the *Risorgimento*; both are concerned with the urgent necessity for Lombardy's freedom from Austrian rule, but this concern has a Catholic colour or cast. Pellico's experiences in the Spielberg prison bear witness to the sublimation of suffering in faith, and it is essentially the same faith linked with justice in a broadly Manzonian formula that sustains Franco in *Il Piccolo mondo antico*. Neither is a novel of the Catholic conscience in the fully Manzonian sense, though both exemplify in different ways that Catholic view of life which was still, perhaps to 1860, a fundamental part of the Italian nineteenth century.

Silvio Pellico emerged from that stable of Italian Romantics, the *Conciliatore*, which had led him to an Austrian prison. He relates his experiences at Spielberg with no driving hate or motive in political vendetta—though the impact of the book was, of course, politically damaging to the Austrian cause—but turns the other cheek and narrates the story of his soul. Historical accuracy (witness the second opinion of Maroncelli) and compassion are his intentions, and produce a formula to evoke Manzoni. Pellico experienced incredible privation and suffering, but arrives, through suffering, at resignation and faith. Perhaps because of its political reticence, a failure to comment on the political realities underlying his historical position, the book still has the power to move and evoke sympathy, for its message is removed from its time by this detachment. *Le Mie prigioni* speaks of injustice first, the consolations of the Catholic faith second, and political domination a poor third. These enduring and moral preoccupations place the work in a line between the writings on justice of Beccaria (who was Manzoni's maternal grandfather) in the eighteenth century and the drama of Ugo Betti in our own time (see p 164). Pellico remains a recorder of experience, a witness to the Catholic conscience rather than a creative artist of genius; possibly his experiences move us more than his way of writing.

ANTONIO FOGAZZARO

If Pellico was the romantic product and victim of his age—that generation of Manzoni and Leopardi which was born before the Revolution—Fogazzaro was far more a child of the complexities of *Risorgimento* Italy. He is often taken to stand between the world of Manzoni at the beginning of the century and that of D'Annunzio at the end of it—the passage from positivism to decadence; but even the title of his most readable novel—*Il Piccolo mondo antico*—is an indication that he is looking back. The central character, Franco, looks back across the battle-scarred years of the middle of that century to the security, the solidity and the relative calm of Manzoni's world. His relationship with his more forward-looking wife, Luisa, is a meeting of the old world and the new—a contrast, almost, of the idealistic patriotism and simple faith of the *garibaldino* years and the disturbing portents (represented by Luisa) of the new century that were already apparent when the book was written in 1895. The Catholic conscience of the work is uncertain, its idealism vague compared with the rock of Manzoni, but even this unease—the failure to resolve completely some of the artistic problems in Fogazzaro's novels—is symbolic of his generation. To an extent, also, the work reflects a deep spiritual malaise, a crisis both spiritual and institutional in Catholicism, suffered by many Italian Catholics of Fogazzaro's generation.

The Church had gone through its own greatest trauma since the Avignonese papacy in the lifetime of Petrarch. Like the annexation of the *Veneto* to the new Italian nation, the winning of Rome was almost an accidental result of outside forces. For the obstacle to the completion of the Italian national map, with its great classical monument in the centre, had been the undertaking given by Cavour to French Catholic opinion. This was why Piedmont had had to block Garibaldi's attempts to take Rome in 1862 and 1867. But then came the Franco-Prussian war in 1870; France, which had been protecting the pope, was defeated at Sedan and Italian troops finally entered Rome by the Porta Pia on 20 September. The events of that day had enormous consequences for Italian Catholic opinion and conscience, not to speak of Catholics outside Italy. The papal state, the visible incarnation of some thousand years of Christian tradition and conscience, had succumbed to Italian force. To add to this turmoil and the intransigence of Pius IX—who refused to allow Catholics to stand for parliament or vote—Fogazzaro's world of 1895, when the novel was written, was characterised by the conflicts caused by liberalism, anti-clericalism and many shades of political opinion. The political diversity of modern Italy was being forged; the Catholic conscience of many people, severely tried so many times between 1848 and 1895, was in tumult, and a new relationship between Church and state was to be gradually constructed over the ensuing years in a process that still continues. It is difficult to see how the visions of Dante, Tasso and Manzoni could ever return now. The disintegration of traditional unities in national, intellectual and spiritual life were more a product of the 1870s than the 1860s, as far as the Catholic conscience and its extensions in literature are concerned. Fogazzaro's novel is only one pointer to this sense of disintegration, and in any case hardly ranks with the great unifying works of the literature of the Catholic conscience.

Il Piccolo mondo antico delineates not only the pre-*Risorgimento* Italy of Austrian political domination; it was also the antique world of Manzoni's Catholicism. The new world emerges in the distance between Franco and Luisa; more rounded than Fogazzaro's other characters, they live out some of the crises of his age. Franco's faith is secure and conventional, based on concrete convictions; the faith of Luisa is a new and disquieting yearning, some loss of the old charity, a dabbling in the occult. In its nostalgic re-evocation of pre-*Risorgimento* values, the novel mirrors the dilemma of many contemporary Catholics; in spite of the title, it is prophetic rather than reflective, looking forward to the twentieth century in the greater relief accorded to the character Luisa. The Catholic conscience as a reality permeating down to the roots of literature, as it were—informing the whole life of art, a vision and a view of life—stopped with Manzoni. We shall find Catholic views in twentieth-century literature, certainly, but the Catholic conscience as a dominant theme perhaps reached its delta with *I Promessi sposi*; we shall look at some streams and tributaries in the final chapter.

Notes to this chapter are on p 176.

CHAPTER 5

The Dissection of Man: the Twentieth Century

The problems caused by the gradual establishment of Italian nationhood and the difficulties experienced by that nation between 1870 and 1900 have already been described (see p 72). Until the turn of the century it has been possible to follow the streams of 'dominant themes' in literature which have run through the history of the Italian people, involving major and minor literary talents to a greater or lesser extent. Sometimes a theme has touched a great writer only lightly, producing a pigeon-hole into which he fits uneasily. Elsewhere, the theme was really dominant in that the writer may be characterised fairly fully by reference to it. In other places, writers exemplify more than one Italian theme, or indeed all of them—as did the great founders of Italian literature: Dante, Petrarch and Boccaccio. Of course, all classification of literature—be it by theme, genre or historical period—must distort finally, since writers are individuals; but the thematic treatment has thrown up, to this point, some dominant preoccupations of Italian writers in 600 years of their history. It is therefore true that every twentieth-century Italian writer carries a consciousness of these preoccupations in his literary equipment; it is part of the character of being a twentieth-century Italian.

Dominant themes are perhaps less useful as categories after Manzoni. Franco Fortini has written of the modern period: 'It is becoming more and more difficult to talk about dominant themes in Italian literature'; and Guido Almansi added, 'there are societies which come to be described as top heavy. Italy is *past-heavy*.'[1] So in this chapter we shall be looking at the fragmentation of themes, some minor expressions of the old major themes and some quite new preoccupations of modern Italy in writing. Italian writers of the twentieth century have turned away from the old major themes, for the most part, and the century began with attempts to seek alternative values inside man himself—hence the chapter title 'The Dissection of Man'.

THE 'DECADENT' PERIOD

That period of crisis and transition in Italian history which spans the end of the nineteenth century and the beginning of the twentieth has often been called 'decadent' in terms of its literature. This tradition, which looks forward, heralds exciting changes and presages some typically twentieth-century themes, is well represented by the works of Luigi Pirandello and Italo Svevo. Pirandello looked behind the façades of life to pose the question: What is real and what is illusory in life, society, human relationships and, indeed, art? Svevo, too, examined the nature of personality, but concentrated in his novels particularly on the problem of the individual.

Why did two major Italian writers seek to expose the problems of the human personality and psychology in the period before and after World War I? In part, writers of Pirandello's and Svevo's generation were reacting against the nineteenth century and its values. European political ideals had disintegrated: nationalism and imperialism were in conflict with the democratic yearnings of Italians; their philosophical counterpart, positivism, that blind faith in man's capacity for progress, was giving way to an irrational view of civilisation and sense of solitude. The first was to lead Europe and Italy inexorably into World War I; the second was to leave writers with a sense of helplessness, of being somehow lost in the sea of life without a secure point of anchorage. All this cannot explain Pirandello and Svevo, but provides some co-ordinates for them—a historical point of reference in time. The Italian negotiator at the Paris peace conference returned with his hands virtually empty of Italian gains. National prestige was at a low ebb, and contrasted starkly with relative prosperity and material expansion before 1914.

LUIGI PIRANDELLO

Into this political and cultural climate of postwar Italy, Pirandello introduced the habit of self-examination; his significant writing, however, goes back to the early years of the century. Far from merely displaying a reaction to the social realism of Verga, the decadent egoism of D'Annunzio and political pessimism, Pirandello ushered in a whole new fashion in literature. This involved a positive change of direction towards an ironical but compassionate view of man in his many states of being, his self-erected façades and barriers, the nature of his personality, the impossibility of communication with his fellows in the uniqueness of every individual, and the relation between life and artistic form. Pirandello projected the all-pervading dualism of illusion and reality through plays, novels and short stories, not only reflecting the bewilderment and disorientation of many Italians in the first twenty years of the century by his retreat, in a sense, into the psyche, into questions of philosophy expressed through art, but also, and positively, founding a tradition to which the twentieth-century theatre owes a demonstrable debt.

Symptomatic of Pirandello's central preoccupations was his greatest play, *Sei personaggi in cerca d'autore*, whose effect on the modern European theatre might be compared with Picasso's

Demoiselles d'Avignon on painting. Six characters, rejected by their author, wander into a theatre in the course of a rehearsal, interrupt the actors, producer and stage hands, claiming priority for their own truer, more real and lived drama over the artificiality and illusory nature of the rehearsal. Throughout the play, Pirandello constantly juxtaposes these two planes of reality; the life of the characters is held up against the artifice of the staged play to produce an almost hallucinatory opposition of art and life. The symbolic divide, the footlights, is crossed and recrossed; space and time are blurred in terms of conventional theatre, and the lines separating the two realities are destroyed when one character, the stepdaughter, flirts with an actor.

The characters are impelled by an internal compulsion to live their drama, which gradually captures and convinces the actors. The actors, in turn, make half-hearted attempts to act the characters' drama, throwing the artificiality of the staged play devastatingly into focus. The problems of identity and communication are powerfully evinced in the character of the father; he complains bitterly that he is something different to all men, and that this fact is tragically at the root of his relations with his wife. A host of minor incidents—the supernatural appearance of Madame Pace, the intrusion of a stage hand, the introduction of real rather than staged death—all contribute to the fragmentation of conventional theatrical form, in the play's constant turning in upon itself. The producer, perhaps a modern Prospero figure, sometimes links the various planes of reality, sometimes divides them, sometimes echoes audience reaction or seems to comment on the whole Pirandellian structure.

The first reaction to such a spectacle may be to observe that this is a game. Pirandello's task in all his major works was the dramatisation of the subconscious. Why then is *Sei personaggi in cerca d'autore*—an attempt to create compelling visual stage art from metaphysical concepts—an artistic success? The answer is that such concepts are nearer than we think; illusion and reality are constituents of everyday experience which generate much of the emotion, hardship, tragedy and failure of everyman, and, as such, are universal. They produced the tragedy of the father in all his pathos and well-meaning but weak affirmations; and the fall of the stepdaughter, a prisoner of her family tragedy and the society which allowed it to happen. They also produced the failure to communicate of all the characters; the almost continuous hysteria of the mother serves to remind the audience that Pirandello's material is not a play on words but the stuff of the home, the desperation of man at odds with his society. Finally, the heartrending fate of the children is almost biblical in its force, the result of the tragedy of their parents in lust, fear, jealousy and incomprehension.

The contrasts between 'being' and 'seeming', between individual and society, between aspiration to truth and justice and that 'mask' which our society or circumstances forces us to wear are central also to Pirandello's best-known novel, *Il fu Mattia Pascal*, which preceded *Sei personaggi* . . ., and was an early working out of some of its themes. But the novel is possibly a less satisfying expression of the debate. The protagonist decides to relinquish his former identity to assume another and make a new start. This initiative is blocked at every turn by a variety of social conventions, showing the individual as a prisoner of the environment into which the world has thrust him. The play *Enrico IV* investigates the problem of madness, sanity being a 'norm' imposed on the individual by society. Enrico IV is forced to feign madness, playing the part imposed on him by circumstances, just as in another of his plays, *Così è se vi pare*, Laudisi, Pirandello's mouthpiece, shows an incredulous bourgeois society how their beliefs in the certainty of evidence are suspect and illusory, each man's view of the situation being the one he most wishes to believe. Through all Pirandello's work runs a current of solitude, of the individual at the mercy of life's circumstances; there is a bitter-sweet irony in the constant juxtaposition of the real and the mask, a harsh stripping away of the illusions in which we all comfortably wrap ourselves as protection from unpalatable truths.

ITALO SVEVO

Svevo, too, searched inside the human personality and, in particular, the consciousness in his three works: *Una vita*, *Senilità* and *La Coscienza di Zeno*, his masterpiece. As with Pirandello, therefore, Svevo's writing turned its back decisively on the nineteenth century, on realism, on those great themes of political, religious and social experience that had run through Italian literature for so long. In part, this was because Svevo was hardly a true Italian—being of mixed German and Italian origins, and living for most of his life in Trieste, a geographical fringe of Italy—but more importantly he was moved to abandon the traditional Italian themes to look under the surface of personality at the subconscious.

La Coscienza di Zeno seems at first about as un-Italian as one could imagine. The novel purports to be an autobiography written in response to instructions from Zeno's psychoanalyst: both a confession and a memoir. But it ironically attacks the whole tradition of confession and autobiography writing, and questions the problem of self-analysis in general and psychoanalysis in particular. Zeno recounts the story of his life, his early days and the traumatic relationship with his father, his constantly unfulfilled ambition to give up smoking, his wavering and indecisive career ambitions, his marriage to the only one of three sisters whom he had not seriously intended to court, his success in business in spite of, rather than because of, his natural talents and so on. The work is a *tour de force* of contradiction of conventional motivations and values. Zeno is the anti-hero of modern Italian literature, the antithesis of the whole apparatus of dominant traits that go to make up the average Italian. Perhaps more than in any other work, *La Coscienza di Zeno* projects the search of the individual for an identity, a niche, a place in the scheme of things which writers of Svevo's generation felt they had lost.

So Italian literature in the first twenty years of the twentieth century broke decisively with the past. Pirandello and Svevo dwelt on the modern and universal problem of individual identity, conscious and subconscious, illusion and reality. They were prophetic in the sense that they reflected the bewilderment of a society in transition, a searching after truth rather than the old convinced statements of it. World War I broke that society finally, the climax of that sense of foreboding that we sense in writers of Svevo's generation. Fascism followed and most really significant writing went underground, to re-emerge after the fall of Mussolini and to re-assume some characteristic Italian forms.

Just as Pirandello and Svevo had broken decisively with traditionally Italian dominant themes, so poets of the inter-war years sought to rid themselves of the apparatus of past traditions, to abandon rhetorical forms and moralising themes, to transmit the suffering of man as a victim of the terrible pressures of World War I and Fascism. That element of renunciation of the past has been called Hermeticism—the retreat of Italian poetry into a world of individually felt emotions and expression. As such, therefore, the break with the past—with dominant themes in all that they imply—parallels the achievements of Pirandello in the theatre and of Svevo in the novel form.

GIUSEPPE UNGARETTI

The best-known exponent of 'Hermetic' poetry is Giuseppe Ungaretti, whose work constitutes a reduction to the barest essentials. His poems are almost random reflections on the war and the sufferings of the individual through the long period—1916–60—of his productivity. This led to his early poems being defined as 'fragments', but also contributed to a sense of the 'essential'—the quintessence—of things that one feels when reading his work; the essence, it should be added, of all things in human experience and aspirations, for the poets of Hermeticism were not bound by Pirandello's intellectual rigour in the philosophical basis for their work. They felt, dreamt and cherished illusion. This latter aspect comes to the fore in Ungaretti's later collection of poems, the *Sentimento del tempo*, in which the Italian countryside returns to poetry, as it were, to provide a lyrical framework, a fuller context, and perhaps a more Italian flavour to the truths the poet expresses, than the earlier harshly skeletal compositions.

EUGENIO MONTALE

The poetry of Eugenio Montale was of the same generation; it built upon, and reacted against, the same foundations in the nineteenth century—Pascoli, D'Annunzio etc—and is symptomatic again of the crisis of a modern Italian. The cruelty of the destiny allotted to man comes across strongly, harsh, unremitting and pessimistic in his 1925 collection, the *Ossi di Seppia*. But the medium is different in substantial aspects from that chosen by Ungaretti. A fuller and more involved poetic style, syntactically complex, made up of strong contrasts and harsh dissonances, projects this pessimism and this sorrow, but also a paradoxical love for life. Perhaps the greatest Italian poet of the twentieth century, Montale seems to translate the existential anguish of today with an Italian verse form that is both universal and European, and yet individually Italian, full of myths and symbols, intellectually satisfying and moving.

SALVATORE QUASIMODO

With Salvatore Quasimodo we come to the first Italian poet actually born in the twentieth century, and the one with whom most anthologies end. He is perhaps incorrectly linked with the

poets of Hermeticism, for Quasimodo's sorrow is for the home-
land of Sicily; the nostalgia and sense of regret are more individually Italian and Sicilian than part of European existentialism.
The music of the Italian language comes back; its sound values
and expressionism contrast with the more concentrated essence
of language used by Ungaretti and Montale. If Ungaretti and
Montale looked across the frontiers of Italy to express the values
of their generation in poetic terms that are both timeless and
international, Quasimodo's vision is a narrower one, assimilating
more fully the lessons of the past, but more regional than national,
more national than individual.

So the Italian poetry of Hermeticism, if the phrase means anything at all, hardly serves to classify the three best-known poets
in Italy who lived through both world wars. A dominant theme
can scarcely be constructed from a renunciation of the concept of
a literary past! But, historically, poets as well as playwrights and
novelists were not left unmarked by the terrible destiny meted
out to them by the present century, and they too, in the flight
from realism, romanticism, verism, or whatever, of their nineteenth-century literary tradition, have their implicit statements to
make about twentieth-century civilisation, just as the present
generation of poets, particuarly Mario Luzi and Vittorio Sereni,
continue to do.

THE MAJOR THEMES IN POSTWAR ITALY

The contribution of the anti-Fascist current of writing between
the wars, and its outcome, the literature of the Resistance, have
been surveyed as the modern extension of the theme of the
Italian political conscience. World War II had an effect on the
Italian people much greater and stronger than that of World War
I, for Italy was in a sense a loser and suffered the indignity of
having to change sides (see p 81). Postwar Italian literature continues to search for a meaning and a national identity. The

tumultuous changes in society; the crisis of moral values; the widespread yearning for radical reforms of ideas and political structures, and the broadening of that society that has become both a producer and a consumer of literature; and severe economic and social problems have all had an indelible effect on the Italian literary scene. Hardly any attempt to generalise about the course of Italian literature since 1945 will satisfy, except to say that it has come home again, so to speak, to mirror and reflect the anxiety and national uncertainty caused by the war, and multiple concerns of a national or local nature.

Those writers we examined for their politically orientated works express a continuing preoccupation with left-wing attitudes as the alternative to fallen Fascism (see p 76). Levi and Silone, who expressed this dualism under Fascism, have continued to do so—Levi until his death in 1975 and Silone until today. Vittorini, Pavese and Calvino, in their different ways, have made their contributions to this process.

ALBERTO MORAVIA

The theme of social change and social criticism has found a writer whose reputation has become international: Alberto Moravia. His novel *Gli Indifferenti*, still considered his masterpiece, appeared as long ago as 1929. It constituted a resounding denunciation of twentieth-century middle-class values, and also embodies a style of writing that reflects everyday speech. In the first of these two areas—social criticism—Moravia's work has had a profound effect; in the second, it has resulted in some devaluation—a playing to the gallery of popular large-scale book consumption—which has brought critical reaction to the later popular works.

Gli Indifferenti recounts the progressive stages of moral degradation of an average Italian middle-class family, Moravia reveals their social conventions, empty of real values; their pathetic inertia, their corruption in moral terms and their arid nothing-ness, their indifference to the world around them. The mother is locked in the prison of her fading charms and nostalgia for youth, behind a thin façade of exterior respectability. The middle-aged friend of the family hides his corrupt influence beneath a mask of charm, apparent disinterestedness and materialism. The daughter is blown this way and that by conflicting loyalties, incapable of decision, initiative and personal integrity. Michele's revolt against mindless conformity with this empty world is a momentary idealism, destined to fade when he slips back into the ugly hole his family has fashioned for him. In the novel that revolt simply hints at an alternative—a break with the corrupting tradition—showing up his family in the true light of their empty lives. Moravia's characters are tragic because of their knowledge of their own state—their self-awareness but total lack of construc-tive initiative.[2] The twin preoccupations of their society, painted by Moravia in his novel, are sex and money—themes which appear again, obsessively, in his later writing and persist in Italian society today.

CARLO CASSOLA

The writings of Carlo Cassola and Giorgio Bassani, which also reflect some realities of present-day Italy, are based in the writers' own memories and impressions. Cassola (see p 87) has become identified since the war with reflections on the Italian middle class, but digs below the surface for motivations, psychology and aspirations in the search for positive values. Bassani is more concerned with external reality and relates rather than researches in a more linear narrative tradition; but both writers show the marks of the war on the Italian. Underlying the works of both Cassola and Bassani are direct experience of the war and its trau-matic effects on literature; they have transferred to the written page the combination of lived experience and the impelling necessity to write, to fix in a literary mode these lived experiences and the emotions they caused. With Cassola, one can follow the development of the author in *Fausto e Anna* through *La Ragazza di Bube*, in the psychological penetration of the character Mara, to *Il Taglio del bosco*. In this last, Cassola is, in a sense, liberated from the nightmare of the war and its effects; he has reacted against them and allowed free rein to his literary rather than to his politico-historical motivations, to produce a bond between characters, events and their Tuscan setting.

GIORGIO BASSANI

Bassani's best-known work is probably *Il Giardino dei Finzi-Contini*, a major novel which has found wide critical acclaim. Typical of the writer in its preoccupation with Ferrara and the problem of the persecution and oppression of Jews, it is profoundly moving, autobiographical and intimate. The work centres on the relationship between the young protagonist with literary ambitions and Micòl, the daughter of a local well-to-do Jewish family. Their meetings—complicated always by the presence of Micòl's brother, Alberto, and their friend, Malnate, and situated symbolically in a socially acceptable environment (the tennis-court)—develop a deep and complex relationship on which the external realities of study for examinations, persecution of Jewish families and the impending war only impinge to lend background and half-tones to this central theme.

The relationship is described with personal involvement, delicacy and refinement, and the realism of the motivations is a telling index of the work's modernity—the solitude, lack of communication, no conclusion. In short, the novel is at once historically valid, psychologically deeply perceptive, and literary in the broadest sense.

The works of Moravia, Cassola and Bassani express in their very different ways the reality of present-day Italian society. They are hardly novels of social change, but portray a deep consciousness of the crises of Italian society. The same is true also of our third major theme: the Catholic conscience. Most Italians today are still conscious that they are Catholics. The Church-and-state debate goes on in Italy as nowhere else. The nineteenth-century struggle of the papacy for its centuries-old territorial status continues in the struggles inherent in a Catholic country with a Communist party growing in political force and influence. The political anti-clericalism of a writer like Carducci in the nineteenth century has become an ideological anti-clericalism of Communists who see the Christian Democrat vote as a religious rather than political choice to be fought.

The works of contemporary writers reflect the enduring fact that the fabric of Italian society is Catholic in a way northern Europeans without direct experience of it often do not understand. The Catholic conscience in Italian society is so entrenched and all-pervading that it may be satirised with success and without offence, and depicted in all the gradations of its relative purity and humanity. Just as Don Abbondio's humanity contrasts with Borromeo's sanctity in *I Promessi sposi*, so the good priest and the bad Prete Cirillo in Emilio de Marchi's *Il Capello del prete* can be juxtaposed each as a foil for the other, the moral lesson obvious. This is a natural constituent in a very minor work, a current inherent in the reflection of almost any Italian society, just as the playful use of the fabric of Catholic society in Guareschi's works has amused an international audience, but is nowhere near a grand theme.

UGO BETTI

With the playwright Ugo Betti we come to Italy's foremost dramatist since Pirandello. His central preoccupations are certainly moral and sometimes implicitly religious. In his most famous plays—*Frana allo scalo nord, L'Aiuola bruciata* and *Corruzione al Palazzo di Giustizia*—Betti exhibits a concern for the dualism of human and divine justice that was the fruit of a legal career. Like Pirandello, Betti shows the moral dilemma of modern man, the difficulty of choice. Human justice, about which Betti's plays speak with the obsession of a professional, is a weak expression of divine justice. The conflicts facing modern man are those between the social and moral desire for harmony, and the individual and selfish desire for self-advancement.

In his *Corruzione al Palazzo di Giustizia*, Betti depicts the trial of magistrates accused of having abused the privileges of their position. The net of culpability also catches the accusers, being themselves not entirely without blame, and widens further to enmesh even the relatives of the inquisitors. Ugo Betti's own legal background is here most clearly in evidence. The corruption of the institution symbolises a universal impossibility of freedom from guilt. No one is immune; even those raised to positions of authority and responsibility—and those raised even higher to inquire into the conduct of that responsibility—carry with them the burden of imperfection, of human error and the pangs of conscience that result.

Frana allo scalo nord is also a play with a legal context and setting: an inquiry into the circumstances of a landslide at a construction site. It portrays the attempt to assess the blame for shoddy work and misconduct, and the unmistakable courtroom framework—the collection of evidence, calling of witnesses, official pronouncements of tired officialdom—is typical of Betti's drama. Self-justification becomes confused with expiation in the emotional statements of witnesses; the contrast between individual human anguish and the legal and scientific search for an absolute and impartial truth from which society must exact its tribute is also strongly marked. The furniture of this courtroom context provides Betti with his confessional; witnesses demonstrate their guilt far beyond the specific events of the inquiry; the judge's mask of impartiality gradually falls away to reveal his own guilt feelings, and the appearance of supernatural witnesses emphasises the universal nature of original sin. In the end, the character of

Parsc comes prominently to the fore in his telling verdict of compassion for human error rather than justice in society's retribution for sin in accordance with defined laws.

In the third of Betti's well-known plays, *L'Aiuola bruciata*, the setting and context are again deliberately unspecific, underlining the questions of principle at the root of the author's preoccupations. As in *Frana allo scalo nord* where the characters have un-Italian, and therefore stateless, names and ranks, so in *L'Aiuola bruciata* the exact nature of the political cause being fought for is obscure. The play appeals for tolerance and moderation in a world torn by strife. It juxtaposes the devotion of men to political causes or ideologies with that to home and family, showing the tragedy that may result when the former replaces the latter. The outcome of political struggle is war, and Betti points out that the duties of political commitment may lead men into conflict for reasons which are trivial and far removed from fundamental human, moral and ethical values. These values, on the other hand, inform the duty to home and family. From these contrasts, Betti draws powerful drama. The death of the small boy is symbolic of this misplaced system of priorities; responsibility is again the key principle of the play: to people or politics? The sacrifice of the innocent Rosa becomes, not the sacrifice to a cause, but the impelling tragedy of humanity betrayed.

ITALIAN LITERATURE TODAY

In the final section of this chapter, it may be appropriate to describe the physiognomy of the present-day Italian. What literature has he been reading since the war? We have been concerned so far with the dominant themes of his literary past and some echoes in his present, but what is he now? He is perhaps just as concerned with the enduring realities of Italian life as were his forbears—with politics, his social state and Catholic conscience—but the literature of present-day Italy also reflects preoccupation with many other modern problems of importance nationally. It uses themes or content patterns which every modern Italian will have argued about in the home, at the office or in the family Fiat on the way to the annual seaside or mountain holiday. Some of the most important issues are the Italian family, the problem of the south, the Mafia, industrialisation and regionalism.

NATALIA GINSBURG

We have noted those characteristics of solidity and durability that go to make up the Italian family (see p 120). A modern exponent of this theme has been Natalia Ginsburg with her widely acclaimed novel, *Lessico famigliare*, published in 1963. Built on a substratum of autobiographical reflections, the work has been seen as 'a sentimental portrait of a whole generation'.[3] It is revealing, particularly to the foreign reader of Italian, as a reflection of those values which characterise Italian families in recent generations. The very title suggests that web of complex relationships which characterises all Italian blood relationships: the special privilege of belonging to the clan, the duty to further the aims of that microcosm of Italian society, and the restraints and boundaries that that duty imposes on the individual—in this example, in middle-class Turin. In *Lessico famigliare* the family of the author's memory and imagination is delicately portrayed, and inspires instant recognition in most northern Italians. The dualism of the father, traditionally paternalistic but everlastingly affectionate, is instantly Italian. His wife combines the qualities of maternal control and a likeable feminine individuality—again, perfectly reconcilable attributes in an Italian mother. The web of relatives extends in all directions, their mutual loyalties fixed, as it were, in the set mould of the Italian family structure, their duties circumscribed first by the sentiment of belonging and only second by exterior circumstances.

It must be obvious by now that *Lessico famigliare* depicts a particular kind of northern family—powerfully intellectual, creative, Jewish—and one that represents, in the full sense, very few typical families in Italy outside a fairly restricted geographical and intellectual milieu. In the novel's particular qualities resides much of its artistic success, as with any significant work. But the constants are there, just as they are in Ginsburg's short story, *La Madre*, a moving account of the tragedy of one family and the innocent sensitivity of small children. One could choose any one of a hundred contemporary works which—in dependence, description, rejection or tragic loss of these central enduring characteristics of the Italian family—fix the theme as a constant constituent, in its infinite gradations, of almost all modern Italian literature.

DANILO DOLCI

The problem of the south and the so-called two civilisations of modern Italy have their roots in historical situations far back in the past. The postwar dimensions of the problem—in the deployment of government resources; the movement of labour, emigration and depopulation; the updating of agricultural methods and the attempt at some industrialisation—have been brought to an international audience by the books of Danilo Dolci. Always a polemicist and consciously committed, Dolci has tried to highlight what he feels to be the injustice of the Sicilian's destiny: inadequately considered in the allocation of national resources, misunderstood by northern Italian prejudice that still runs deep, and hampered by the historical disadvantages of slowness to adapt to new conditions, lack of initiative and the stranglehold of the Mafia. Of course, Dolci writes exclusively about a problem, and as such it must have at least two sides. But the passion of commitment and the devotion of compassion—in equal measure, perhaps—lend conviction to Dolci's writing, which, though it may be less gifted in a literary sense than that of Levi and Silone, is a telling witness to what can be done to redress social evils, provided that one perseveres in the face of all opposition.

In his attempt to remedy the sociological wounds from which Sicily suffers, Dolci's life has been devoted to non-violent opposition to all forms of bureaucracy and officialdom. His zeal has been missionary, sociological and political, and his books are fired with the enthusiasm of the prophet, social worker and fifth columnist. In *Banditi a Partinico*, possibly his best-known, the people themselves speak of their misery; the author describes his attempts to make them aware of their plight, while officialdom and the Mafia are implicitly condemned. Through this and Dolci's other works, similarly orientated and equally polemical, the radical view of the problem of the south emerges. The sociological divergence between southern economic hardship and cultural poverty, and the relative prosperity of the industrialised north, is stated with conviction to an international audience. Dolci's books are a telling document, not a literary monument. Their popularity bears witness to a broadening European consciousness of sociological deprivation. What was a Bourbon problem some hundred years ago is an Italian problem in a unified nation. Where underdeveloped regions are increasingly on the agenda of European discussions, an awareness, at least, of some of the complexities of the problem of the south has been facilitated by Dolci's writing.

LEONARDO SCIASCIA

Reflecting part of the southern problem has been the growing body of literature which takes the Mafia as its theme. This phenomenon—rooted primarily, though not exclusively, in the south—combines some of the literary themes we have been describing, in a very particularised manifestation of them. The southern Italian family remains somewhat less susceptible to the Europeanising influences of the north; and it retains paternal domination and the subjection of the woman—though this general tendency is changing fast. The web of family duties and loyalties which might characterise Ginsburg's Turin is more darkly and deeply etched, remains more self-centred and carries more weight, socially, in Palermo. Thus the twin concepts of *vendetta* and *omertà* are the transposition of the values of a northern Italian family into the harsh colours and stark contrasts of southern society.[4] The Mafia is generally recognised as an organisation —highly sophisticated and developed in international gangster networks and illegal commercial or trafficking enterprises—which trades on the strength of these old family values in the south. The Mafia itself has all the hallmarks of a family. Thus, offences against family taboos, deflowering of virgins, and the rivalries of gangs competing for conflicting business interests result in murder, extortion and blood feuds. The career of the bandit Giuliano is the best-publicised example of this kind of drama, opening the door to a legendary status similar to that of criminal elements in the American West.

So, as with the literature of the Resistance and of the Cold War, the Mafia is gradually acquiring its own school of writers who use the dramatic colours of such situations in their work. The novel *Il Giorno della civetta*, by the widely respected Sicilian writer, Leonardo Sciascia, may be taken as a good example of this type. Devoted to the context, colours and drama of Sicilian society, Sciascia successfully dramatises one of the most ingrained and widely publicised aspects of southern Italian society. The novel not only describes the existence and practice of the Mafia as a criminal organisation, but with observation and psychological penetration it also builds fully rounded characters, full-toned backgrounds to reflect its social causes and effects. The book is both a portrait of Sicily—believable, human, in places deliciously funny—and an eloquent condemnation of the inability of authority to eradicate a social evil. As a portrait of the Mafia, its accuracy is undoubted; the interaction of characters is expertly managed and the north/south contrast of the wider Italian context is brought firmly into focus.

The novel describes the efforts of a police officer from the north to arrest and convict those guilty of a Mafia-type double murder. The evidence is uncovered; suspects are questioned. Gradually the network of relationships between members of 'The Honoured Society'—the oldest of all Sicilian families—extends to involve figures of social standing and importance. At this point, the suspects—backed by highly placed friends and impeccable but fabricated alibis, and aided by the eyewitnesses' fear of reprisal—are freed through 'lack' of evidence; confessions previously 'extorted' are retracted, and the case for the prosecution folds up. 'There is no such thing as the Mafia,' everyone says, 'simply another example of northern prejudice.' The writing and characterisation are compelling and entertaining; but the book also tellingly documents the mores and values of Sicilian society from the standpoint of a native writer.

OTTIERO OTTIERI

Industry and technology, the results of Italy's postwar economic miracle, have produced a new sector of experience which is being increasingly utilised by the Italian writer. Since Vittorini originally proposed the theme in 1961, few writers have remained untouched by the values and experiences of the Italian worker suddenly thrust into the framework of industrialisation from a predominantly agriculturally based working life.[5] The effects on such a man of modern factory conditions, the trades union movement and the cooperative principle of collective enterprise in a consumer-orientated society are for the Italian writer a comparatively recent source for drama, anguish and tragedy. One example is given here of the modern theme of industry—which can be followed through far more fully elsewhere.[6]

Ottiero Ottieri is the writer most fully representative of the theme in that he has dedicated himself to it more completely than have his contemporaries. His *Donnarumma all'assalto* is set on the shop floor of an Olivetti factory—a fairly typical Italian industrial situation except that the factory is located in the south, and the north/south conflict deepens the colours of the novel. The workers are correspondingly less well prepared for the shift from the land to a modern factory situation than, say, might be the case in the industrial north; but such regional distinctions are ceasing to mean very much in the constant migration of southern Italians to what they consider the golden work opportunities of northern industrial cities. The southern setting only serves to sharpen the contrast, heighten the drama and deepen the sense of disorientation that Ottieri's factory worker feels. The author's experience—on the management side at Olivetti—undoubtedly assisted him in his task, and the atmosphere of the shop floor is fully expressed through the idiom of the workers themselves. If Ottieri lacked direct experience of the worker's problems, at least his close association with them has lent conviction, authenticity and sympathy to the situations he portrays.

GRAZIA DELEDDA

The literature of the Italian regions—a legacy of pre-*Risorgimento* separateness as much as post-*Risorgimento* regionalism—has been very much alive ever since the appearance of the famous novels of Giovanni Verga, with their specifically Sicilian orientation. Since then, Silone has written novels set in the Abruzzi; Francesco Jovine's writing deals chiefly with the Molise, and Pier Paolo Pasolini adopted Rome, where the important works of Carlo Emilio Gadda are also set. Grazia Deledda has become one of the foremost novelists to bring her region—Sardinia—to the eyes of an international public, her novel *Canne al Vento*,[7] published in 1913, being widely read.

In Deledda's novel the harsh contrasts of the Sardinian countryside and the folklore and superstition of its inhabitants come alive as the real protagonists of the book. Efix, the old retainer of the Pintor sisters, represents the continuity of feudal loyalties to a decaying aristocracy; Lia, a member of the *ancien régime* who succeeded in escaping from it, links the forms and stylised attitudes of an old Sardinian order with the new attractions of the twentieth century, showing the inherent contrast. Giacinto, the lost nephew of the sisters, returns from the world outside to trouble and upset a fixed social order, with its own values, superstitions and folklore; but he also defines that order for the reader. The Sardinian blend of family honour, static social divisions and economic hardship, and the scenic contrasts of sterile land, mountain passes and primitive roads, are all evoked with a passionate devotion to accuracy of detail. Motivations and setting, characters and background produce a reality that is convincingly Sardinian. The dialogues between duty and opportunity, love and death, crime and expiation are worked into this fabric to become natural, almost inevitable constituents of the atmosphere of primitive Sardinia at the beginning of the twentieth century. *Canne al Vento* is a worthy example of Italian regional literature where the local situation and traditions are revealed to the foreign reader with impassioned accuracy and love, while the more universal themes sustain the narrative, characterisation and drama as a novel of our time.

CONTRASTS OF THE PRESENT DAY

Our survey ends with some themes in literature which are pressing and present in the Italy of today. The literature of the regions maintains its strength, expressing that geographical sense of belonging familiar to all who know Italy. This bond also comes through in the continuing fascination of many Italians for not only the local football team but for local history in the many *atti* and *commentari* that embody regional interests and survive the attacks of economic pressures. Dialect poets struggle on, their efforts sustained by a perhaps diminishing regional following, while the dialects themselves are far too deeply rooted to be disturbed by a hundred years of mass-media standardisation.

Industrialisation continues, labour disputes are a daily feature of the national press, and the north has not yet made it up with the south. The Common Market's butter mountains are, for the Italian, orange mounds and tomato tips; and the EEC Common Agricultural Policy has not yet prevented that heart-rending expedient of good and cheap wine being turned into industrial alcohol.

In Italian literature, the old themes and content patterns change and become diffused, but stock values are still present. The priest, influential and almost inevitable, occupies a traditional place in a novel's community, though beset by new problems. The life of an Italian family still revolves round its children, and the love of a mother for her son is as old a theme, religious or social, as the Italian people themselves, and constantly recurs in even the most recent writing. Political and social themes are as much in evidence as they have ever been; Fascism and Communism have been juxtaposed as alternatives in the lifetime and direct experience of all older Italians alive today; and the social fabric of Italian society is still family—locally or regionally orientated—in immediate contrast with the collective principle of association, club and pressure group of many northern Europeans.

As these words were written, Montale had won the Nobel Prize for Literature, the first foreign national was kidnapped for ransom by an Italian gang, and Italian designs at the Paris and London motor shows were recognised for their inimitable style. The civilisation of the Italians is rich in such contrasts, and the literature of her people will doubltess continue to reflect themes old and new, drawing on those values which are individual to the peninsula.

Notes to this chapter are on p 176–7.

Notes

Chapter 1: THE ITALIAN HERITAGE

1 Carlo Salinari. *Profilo storio della letteratura italiana*, I (Rome, 1972), 103
2 The 'Sonnets against the Avignonese papacy', nos 136–8 in the *Canzoniere*. The residence of the pope in Avignon (1305–78) almost exactly coincides with Petrarch's lifespan

Chapter 2: THE POLITICAL CONSCIENCE

1 Niccolò Machiavelli. *Il Principe*, chap 26
2 The distinction, in its application to the modern novel, in Irving Howe's *Politics and the Novel* (New York, 1967), p 27, between the political and social novel is rather different: Howe's field of observation was the novel in various countries, whereas we are considering Italian literature. Thus the distinction between political conscience and social change seems more convenient to our present purposes
3 Cf *L'Arte della guerra, passim; Il Principe*, 6, 18; *Discorsi*, II, 21, etc
4 *Discorsi*, I, 5
5 *Discorsi*, I, 47, 58, III, 29, 34, 59
6 Benvenuto Cellini. *Autobiography*, trans George Bull (Penguin, 1961)
7 Luigi Russo. 'Foscolo politico', in *Belfagor* (1947), 139

Chapter 3: SOCIAL CHANGE

1 Social change is considered here as a theme, a current of content and attitudes, not a cause or foundation of literature; for this latter view (not mine) see David Craig. *The Real Foundations: Literature and Social Change* (London, 1973)

2 More readily accessible are the *Reduce, Bilora* and *Menego*, in a modernised version, in *Dialoghi* (Einandi, 1953)

3 Giovanni Verga. *Pane Nero and other stories*, ed D. Maxwell White (Manchester UP, 1965), 13–14

4 Napoleone Colajanni (1847–1921). *Gli avvenimenti in Sicilia e le loro cause* (Palermo, 1896). This work, as a source for the novel, is argued convincingly by Pieter de Meijer in 'Una fonte de *I Vecchi e i giovani*', *Rassegna di Letteratura Italiana*, VII (1963)

Chapter 4: THE CATHOLIC CONSCIENCE

1 Giovanni Getto recognised that this literature has not been studied in sufficient depth. For the most recent treatment, see his *Letteratura religiosa*, 2 vols (Florence, 1967). The works of St Catherine of Siena are a typical example

2 Christopher Dawson. *Religion and Culture* (London, 1948), 201

3 XII, 65–93. This contrast was pointed out by Mario Fubini in 'La poesia del Tasso', *Studi sulla letteratura del Rinascimento* (Florence, 1971), 282–3

4 The 'new spirituality' is difficult to define in a word; for the best recent study of this aspect of the Counter-Reformation, see H. Outram Evenett. *The Spirit of the Counter Reformation* (Cambridge, 1968)

5 Albert Moravia. *L'uomo come fine* . . . quoted by S. Pacifici. *The Modern Italian Novel* . . . (Carbondale, 1967), 40 etc

Chapter 5: THE DISSECTION OF MAN: THE TWENTIETH CENTURY

1 *20th Century Studies*, V (1971), 18, 4. These authors refer to post-war Italy

2 Perhaps only Moravia's novel *La Noia* (1960) has similar validity

as social criticism combined with artistic success although *La Ciociara* (1957) has met wide critical success and popularity

3 Geno Pampaloni. 'La Nuova letteratura' in *Storia letteraria d'Italia*, IX (Garzanti, Milan, 1969), 868

4 *Omertà*: conspiracy of silence in the criminal underworld, often on the part of eyewitnesses to crime who fear reprisal. It can be seen as an extreme form of Italian family loyalty (in a southern context) to the all-powerful, protective and authoritarian 'family' of the Mafia.

5 See no 4 of the review *Menabò, passim*, but particularly Vittorini's contribution

6 The works of Calvino, Testori, Bianciardi and even Pratolini exemplify this theme, as well as Vittorini himself. Among present-day exponents, Arpino Volponi (*Memoriale*, 1962) and Parise deal with industrial themes

7 Grazia Deledda. *Canne al Vento*, ed M. F. M. Meiklejohn (Manchester UP). First published in 1913, it is hardly representative of *postwar* Italy; but its established popularity and the relative linearity of the author's chosen style have recommended it as an example of modern regional Italian literature

Bibliography

GENERAL

Dizionario della letteratura contemporanea (Valecchi, 1973)
Italian Poetry: a selection from St Francis to Quasimodo, ed and trans Luciano Rebay (Remploy, 1971)
Italian Poets of the Renaissance, ed and trans Joseph Tusiani (New York, 1971)
Letteratura Italiana (Laterza). Multi-volume series
Orientamenti Culturali: I Maggiori, I Minori, I Contemporanei, Le Correnti, I Critici, multi-vol series (Marzoranti, Milan)
The Oxford Book of Italian Verse, ed Carlo Dionisotti (Oxford, 1952)
Pacifici, S. (ed). *From 'Verismo' to Experimentalism* (Indiana UP, 1969)
———. *A Guide to Contemporary Italian Literature* (Meridian Books, 1962)
The Penguin Book of Italian Verse, ed and trans George Kay (Penguin, 1960)
Storia della letteratura italiana, 9 vol (Garzanti, Milan, 1969)
Whitfield, J. H. *A Short History of Italian Literature* (Penguin, 1960)
Wilkins, E. H. *A History of Italian Literature*, rev Bergin (Harvard UP, 1974)

AUTHORS' WORKS AND BIBLIOGRAPHIES

Alfieri, Vittorio (1749–1803)
Scritti politici e morali, ed P. Cazzani (Asti, 1951)
Della Tirannide, trans J. A. Molinaro and Beatrice Corrigan (Toronto UP, 1961)
Del Principe e delle lettere, trans Molinaro/Corrigan (Toronto UP, 1972)

Autobiography: *Vita scritta da esso*, ed E. R. Vincent (Oxford UP, 1961)

The Life of Vittorio Alfieri written by himself, trans H. MacAnally (Kansas UP, 1953)

Gaudence Negaro. *Vittorio Alfieri, Forerunner of Italian Nationalism* (Columbia UP, 1930)

Alighieri, Dante (1265–1321)

The Divine Comedy, 3 vol, ed Natalino Sapegno (Le nuova Italia, Florence, 1955)

—— 3 vol, trans Dorothy L. Sayers and Barbara Reynolds (Penguin, 1960)

—— 3 vol, trans J. D. Sinclair (Oxford UP, 1971)

Inferno, 2 vol, trans Charles S. Singleton (Princeton, 1970)

Umberto Cosmo. *A Handbook to Dante Studies*, trans David Moore (Blackwell, Oxford, 1950)

Dorothy L. Sayers. *Introductory Papers on Dante* and *Further Papers on Dante* (Methuen, 1954, 1957)

Charles Singleton. *Dante Studies* (Harvard UP, 1954)

Michele Barbi. *Life of Dante*, trans P. G. Ruggiers (California UP, 1954)

U. Limentani (ed). *The Mind of Dante* (Cambridge, 1965)

Bassani, Giorgio (1916–)

Il Giardino dei Finzi-Contini (Einaudi); trans Isobel Quigley as *The Garden of the Finzi-Contini* (Ballantine, 1965)

See *Dizionario della lett ital contemp*, I, 102–3; *Orient Cult* (*Contemp*, III)

Beolco, Angelo: 'Il Ruzzante' (1502–42)

Nino Borsellino. *Gli Anticlassicisti del cinquecento* (Lettera Laterza, 20, Rome-Bari, 1973), 141–2

Betti, Ugo (1892–1953)

Frana allo scalo nord and *L'Aiuolo bruciata*, ed G. H. McWilliam (Manchester UP, 1965); trans in Betti, *Three Plays* (Gollancz, 1956); *Frana . . .*, trans G. H. McWilliam in *Three Plays on Justice* (San Francisco, 1964)

Corruzione al palazzo di giustizia, ed Vincent Luciani (Vanni, NY, 1961); trans Henry Reed in *Classics of the Modern Theatre: Realism and After*, ed A. B. Kernen (HarBrace J., 1965)

Boccaccio, Giovanni (1313–75)

Decameron, 2 vol, ed Vittore Branca (Le Monnier, Florence, 1960); trans G. H. McWilliam (Penguin, 1972)

Vittore Branca. *Boccaccio, the Man and his Works* (New York, 1976)

Carlo Segre. *Introduzione al Decameron* (Milan, 1963)

Giovanni Getto. *Vita di forme e forme di vita nel Decameron* (Turin, 1956)

R. Hastings. *Nature and Reason in the Decameron* (Manchester UP, 1975)

A. Scaglione. *Nature and Love in the Late Middle Ages* (California UP, 1963)

G. H. McWilliam. *Boccaccio* (Edinburgh UP, forthcoming)

Bracco, Roberto (1862–1943)

Plays (Mondadori, BMM); *Il Piccolo Santo*, ed V. Luciani (SF Vanni, NY, 1961)

See *Dizionario* . . . (Valecchi, 1973), I, 371

Calvino, Italo (1923–)

Novels (Einaudi paperbacks)

Il Sentiero dei nidi di Ragno, trans A. Colquhoun as *The Path to the Nest of Spiders* (Boston, 1957)

John Woodhouse. *Italo Calvino: a reappraisal and an appreciation of the trilogy* (Hull UP, 1968); Idem (ed). *Il barone rampante* (Manchester UP, 1970)

Capuana, Luigi (1835–1915)

Il Marchese di Roccaverdina, ed Ceriello (Garzanti, Milan, 1958)

L. Bolzoni and M. Tedeschi. *Dalla Scapigliatura al verismo* (Lett Ital Laterza, 1955)

G. Carsaniga. 'Luigi Capuana: from *Verismo* to Idealism' in *The Age of Realism* (Penguin, 1974)

Carducci, Giosuè (1835–1907)

Poems: *Oxford Book of Italian Verse* (1952); *Penguin* . . . (1960)

Le tre corone, poesie e prose: Carducci/Pascoli/D'Annunzio, ed Augusto Vicinelli (Mondadori, 1969)

Rosario Contarino and Rosa Maria Monastra. *Carducci e il tramonto del classicismo* (Lett Ital Laterza), 53

Cassola, Carlo (1917–)

Fausto e Anna, trans Isobel Quigley (Pantheon, 1960)

Frank Rosengarten, 'The Italian Resistance Novel (1945–62)', in *From 'Verismo' to Experimentalism*, ed Pacifici (Indiana UP, 1969)

Castiglione, Baldassare (1478–1529)

Il Cortegiano, ed B. Maier (UTET); trans George Bull as *The Book of the Courtier* (Penguin, 1968); Sir Thomas Hoby, 1561 version (Dent, 1974)

John Woodhouse, *Castiglione* (Edinburgh UP, forthcoming)

Marcello Aurigemma. *Lirica poemi trattati civili del cinquecento* (Lett Laterza), 19, 215–17

D'Annunzio, Gabriele (1863–1938)
Poems (anthologies, see above)
A. Rhodes. *D'Annunzio, the Poet as Superman* (New York, 1960)
H. James. 'G. D'Annunzio', in *Selected Literary Criticism* (Penguin, 1968)
J. R. Harrison. *The Reactionaries* (New York, 1967)

Deledda, Grazia (1871–1936)
Canne al vento, ed M. F. M. Meiklejohn (Manchester UP): see also for selected articles and books, and *Orient Cult* (*Contemp*, I)

Dolci, Danilo (1924–   )
Inchiesta a Palermo, trans P. D. Cummins as *Report from Palermo* (Viking, 1970)
Spreco, trans P. D. Cummins as *Poverty in Sicily* (Penguin, 1966); trans R. Munroe as *Waste* (Monthly Revue, 1964)
Banditi a partinico (Laterza)
See *Dizionario . . .*, 305–6

Fogazzaro, Antonio (1842–1911)
Il Piccolo mondo antico, ed Piero Nardi (Mondadori, 1963)
A. Piromalli in *Orient Cult* (*Minori*, 4), 2987–3038

Foscolo, Ugo (1778–1827)
Ultime lettere di Jacopo Ortis, trans D. Radcliff-Umstead as *Last Letters of Jacopo Ortis* (N Carolina UP, 1970)
Dei Sepolcri, trans T. G. Bergin as *On Sepulchres* (Bethany Press, 1971)
E. R. Vincent. *Ugo Foscolo: an Italian in Regency England* (Cambridge UP, 1953)
D. Radcliff-Umstead. *Ugo Foscolo* (New York, 1970)

St Francis (1181–1226)
Cantico (see anthologies, p 178); trans in *Penguin Book . . .*
J. Jörgensen. *St Francis of Assisi* (Doubleday Image Books)
See *Orient Cult* (*Minori*, I), 23–6

Ginsburg, Natalia (1916–   )
Lessico famigliare (Einaudi); trans D. M. Low as *Family Sayings* (Hogarth, 1967)
See *Orient Cult* (*Contemp*, III) and *Dizionario . . .*, I

Goldoni, Carlo (1707–93)
Il Ventaglio, *La Locandiera* and *Il Bugiardo* (Biblioteca Universale Rizzoli); trans. F. Davies as *The Fan* (Heinemann, 1968); *Mirandolina* in Goldoni, *Four Comedies* (Penguin, 1968), and *The Liar*

(Heinemann, 1963). *La Locandiera* and *Il Ventaglio*, trans Clifford Box, in Goldoni, *Three Comedies* (Oxford UP, 1961)

A. Nicoll. *The World of Harlequin: a critical study of the Commedia dell'Arte* (Cambridge, 1963)

Guido Nicastro. *Goldoni* . . . (Lett Ital Laterza, 37), 79–83

Lampedusa, Giuseppe Tomasi di (1896–1957)

Il Gattopardo (Feltrinelli); trans A. Colquhoun as *The Leopard* (Collins, London, 1960); both in paperback edns

See *Two Stories and a Memory*, trans A. Colquhoun (London, 1962)

G. P. Samonà. *Il Gattopardo* (Florence, 1974)

Leopardi, Giacomo (1798–1837)

Canti (Manchester UP, 1967); trans G. L. Bickersteth as *The Poems of Leopardi* (Russell & Russell, NY, 1973)

Iris Origo. *Leopardi, a study in solitude* (London, 1953)

J. H. Whitfield. *Giacomo Leopardi* (Oxford, 1954)

Levi, Carlo (1902–75)

Cristo si è fermato a Eboli (Mondadori and Einaudi); ed P. M. Brown (Harrap, 1965); trans Frances Frenaye as *Christ Stopped at Eboli* (FS and G, 1947)

M. Miccinesi. *Invito alla lettura di Carlo Levi* (Milan, 1973)

See *Orient Cult* (*Contemp*, III)

Machiavelli, Niccolò (1469–1527)

Il Principe, trans George Bull as *The Prince* (Penguin, 1961); trans C. E. Detmold (WSP, 1970)

Discorsi sopra la prima deca di Tito Livio, trans L. J. Walker as *The Discourses* (Penguin, 1972)

Federico Chabod. *Machiavelli and the Renaissance*, trans David Moore (Harper, 1965)

Felix Gilbert. *Machiavelli and Guicciardini, Politics and History in Sixteenth Century Florence* (Princeton UP, 1965)

J. R. Hale. *Machiavelli and Renaissance Italy* (Pelican, 1972)

Sydney Anglo. *Machiavelli, a dissection* (Paladin, 1971)

J. W. Allen. *A History of Political Thought in the Sixteenth Century* (London, 1951)

Manzoni, Alessandro (1785–1873)

I Promessi sposi, trans A. Colquhoun as *The Betrothed* (Dutton and Dent, 1968); trans Bruce Penman (Penguin, 1972)

S. B. Chandler. *Alessandro Manzoni, the Story of a Spiritual Quest* (Edinburgh UP, 1974)

A. Colquhoun. *Manzoni and his Times, a Biography of the author of 'The Betrothed'* (London, 1954)

Montale, Eugenio (1896–   )
Selected Poems, ed G. Singh (Manchester UP, 1975)
G. Singh. *Eugenio Montale: a critical study of his poetry, prose and criticism* (Yale UP, 1973)
G. Almansi. *Montale* (Edinburgh UP, forthcoming)
See Pacifici. *A Guide . . .*, 177–87

Moravia, Alberto (1907–   )
Gli Indifferenti, trans Angus Davidson as *A Time of Indifference* (Penguin, 1970)
La Noia, trans A. Davidson as *The Empty Canvas* (Penguin, 1965)
La Ciociara, trans A. Davidson as *Two Women* (Secker & Warburg, 1970)
R. W. B. Lewis. 'Alberto Moravia: Eros and Existence' in Pacifici, *From 'Verismo' . . .*, 29–56
D. Heiney. *Three Italian Novelists: Moravia, Pavese, Vittorini* (Michigan UP, 1968)
G. Dego. *Moravia* (Writers and Critics series, NY, 1967)

Ottieri, Ottiero (1924–   )
Donnarumma all'assalto (Bompiani); trans I. M. Rawson as *The Men at the Gate* (London, 1962)
See *Dizionario . . .*, 548

Parini, Giuseppe (1729–99)
Giuseppe Savola. *Parini e la poesia arcadica* (Lett Ital Laterza, 1934)

Pascoli, Giovanni (1855–1912)
Poems (anthologies, as above)
Le tre corone, poesie e prose: Carducci/Pascoli/D'Annunzio, ed Augusto Vicinelli (Mondadori, 1969)

Pavese, Cesare (1908–50)
Il Carcere, trans W. J. Strachan as *The Political Prisoner* (Peter Owen, 1969)
Il Compagno, trans W. J. Strachan as *The Comrade* (Peter Owen, 1959)
La Casa in collina, trans W. J. Strachan as *The House on the Hill* (Peter Owen, 1956; Walker, 1961)
Gian-Paolo Biasin. *The Smile of the Gods* (Cornell UP, 1968)
'Myth and Death in Cesare Pavese's *The Moon and the Bonfire*' in Pacifici *From Verismo . . .*
Donald Heiney. *Three Italian Novelists: Moravia, Pavese, Vittorini* (Michigan UP, 1968)

Pellico, Silvio (1789–1854)

Le mie prigioni (Opera scelte, UTET, Turin, 1954; paperback, BUR, 1953)

Carlo Curto in *Orient Cult* (*Minori*, III), 2411–12

Petrarca, Francesco (1304–74)

Canzoniere, ed Gianfranco Contini (Sansoni, Florence, 1957)

Petrarch, Selected Poems, ed T. Gwynfor Griffith and P. R. J. Hainsworth (Manchester UP, 1971)

J. H. Whitfield. *Petrarch and the Renascence* (Oxford, 1943)

E. H. Wilkins. *Life of Petrarch* (Chicago, 1961); *The Making of the Canzoniere and other Petrarchan studies* (Rome, 1951); *Studies in the life and works of Petrarch* (Cambridge, Mass, 1955)

Umberto Bosco. *Francesco Petrarca* (Bari, 1961)

Carlo Calcaterra. 'Il Petrarca e il Petrarchismo' in *Problemi e orientamenti di letteratura Italiana*, ed A. Momigliano, III (Milan, 1949)

Leonard Forster. *The Icy Fire, five studies in European Petrarchism* (Cambridge UP, 1969)

Pirandello, Luigi (1867–1936)

Sei personaggi in cerca d'autore, trans Frederick May as *Six Characters in Search of an Author* (Heinemann, 1958)

Enrico IV, trans F. May as *Henry IV* in *Penguin Plays* (PL-30) (Penguin, 1962)

Three Plays, ed Felicity Firth (Manchester UP)

Giudice. *Biography of Pirandello*, trans A. Hamilton (Oxford UP, 1975)

T. Bishop. *Pirandello and the French Theatre* (London /NY, 1960)

D. Vittorini. *The Drama of Luigi Pirandello* (New York, 1957)

Olga Ragusa. *Luigi Pirandello* (London/NY, 1968)

——. *Pirandello* (Edinburgh UP, forthcoming)

Pratolini, Vasco (1913–)

Cronache di poveri amanti (Mondadori); trans as *A Tale of Poor Lovers* (New York, 1949)

Frank Rosengarten, *Vasco Pratolini, the development of a social novelist* (Carbondale, 1965)

Pacifici. 'Vasco Pratolini' in *A Guide* . . .

Quasimodo, Salvatore (1901–68)

Tutte le poesie (Mondadori, 1965, 1969); trans Jack Bevan, *Selected Poems* (Penguin, 1970)

C. L. Golino. *Contemporary Italian Poetry*, trans A. Mandelbaum (California UP, 1962), 176–91

See Pacifici. *A Guide* . . ., and *The Penguin Book* . . .

Roberto, Federico de (1861–1927)

I Vicerè, trans A. Colquhoun as *The Viceroys* (London, 1962)

See *Orient Cult* (*Minori*, IV), 3364–71

Sciascia, Leonardo (1921–)

Il giorno della civetta (Einaudi)

See *Dizionario* . . ., I, 706–7

Silone, Ignazio (1900–)

Pane e vino, trans Harvey Fergusson as *Bread and Wine* (Atheneum, 1962)

Uscita di sicurezza, trans H. Fergusson as *Emergency Exit* (Harrow, 1968; Gollancz, 1969); trans William Weaver as *School for Dictators* (Gollancz, 1964)

Fontamara, ed J. A. Rawson (Manchester UP, forthcoming)

Irving Howe. *Politics and the Novel* (New York, 1967)

R. W. B. Lewis. *The Picaresque Saint* (Lippincott, NY, 1959)

Irving Howe. 'Ignazio Silone . . .' in Pacifici, *From Verismo* . . .

Svevo, Italo (1861–1928)

La Coscienza di Zeno, trans Beryl de Zoete as *Confessions of Zeno* (Secker & Warburg, 1962)

P. N. Furbank. *Italo Svevo: the Man and the Writer* (London, 1966)

B. Moloney. *Italo Svevo* (Edinburgh UP, 1974)

J. Freccero. 'Svevo's last cigarette', in Pacifici, *From Verismo* . . ., 35–60

Pacifici. 'I. Svevo's antiheroes' in *The Modern Italian Novel*, 149–83, 191–2

Tasso, Torquato (1544–95)

Gerusalemme liberata, trans Edward Fairfax as *Jerusalem Delivered* (Centaur, 1962; Putnam, 1963); trans Joseph Tusiani (Fairleigh Dickinson UP, USA, 1970)

C. P. Brand. *Torquato Tasso, A Study of the poet and of his contribution to English Literature* (Cambridge UP, 1965)

P. M. Brown. *Tasso* (Edinburgh UP, forthcoming)

Todi, Jacopone da (c 1230–1306)

Poems (anthologies as above)

Giorgio Petrocchi. 'La letteratura religiosa' in *Storia della lett ital* . . ., I, 627–85

See *Orient cult* (*Minori*, I), 147–57

Ungaretti, Giuseppe (1888–1970)

106 poesie, 1914–60 (Mondadori, 1969)

Selected Poems, trans Patrick Creagh (Penguin, 1971)

Pacifici. *The Promised Land and other Poems* (Saba, Ungaretti, Montale and Quasimodo) (Vanni, NY, 1957)

Vita d'un uomo, trans A. Mandelbaum as *Life of a Man* (New Directions, 1958)

Pacifici. *A Guide* . . ., 150–208

F. J. Jones. *Ungaretti* (Edinburgh UP, forthcoming)

Verga, Giovanni (1840–1922)

Pane Nero and other stories, ed D. Maxell White (Manchester UP, 1962)

I Malavoglia, ed M. D. Woolf (Manchester UP); trans R. Rosenthal as *The House by the Medlar Tree* (NAL, 1964)

Mastro-don Gesualdo, trans D. H. Lawrence (Penguin, 1970)

T. Bergin. *Giovanni Verga* (Yale UP, 1931)

A. Alexander. *Giovanni Verga, A great writer and his world* (London, 1972)

Pacifici. 'The tragic world of Verga's primitives' in *From Verismo* . . .

F. W. J. Hennings (ed). *The Age of Realism* (Penguin, 1974), 323–55, 401

Vittorini, Elio (1907–66)

Conversazione in Sicilia, ed R. C. Powell (Manchester UP, forthcoming); trans Wilfred Davies as *Conversation in Sicily* (Drummond, London, 1949)

Donald Heiney. 'Elio Vittorini: the operatic novel' in Pacifici, *From Verismo* . . .

Donald Heiney. *Three Italian Novelists* (Michigan UP, 1968)

Pacifici. 'Elio Vittorini' in *A Guide* . . .

Index of Names

Page numbers in *italics* refer to extended treatment of the author's works in the text. Characters in works of literature are not indexed.